Cultivating A Generous Church

How To Inspire Congregational Generosity and Increase Weekly Offerings

A collection of articles and insight by Mike G. Williams & Jack Eason

CULTIVATING A GENEROUS CHURCH
How To Inspire Congregational Generosity and Increase Weekly Offerings

A collection of articles and insights
by Mike G. Williams and Jack Eason

ISBN: 978-1-951340-00-1
Copyright © 2019
Cover Design by Gerald Brown

For more information about the authors, visit:
www.MikeWilliams.tv
www.theheartsharegroup.com

Many scripture quotations are taken from THE HOLY BIBLE
NEW INTERNATIONAL VERSION® NIV ® Copyright ©
1973, 1978, 1984 by International Bible Society. Used by
permission of Zondervan Publishing House. All rights reserved.

Library of Congress Cataloging-in-Publication Data
Eason, Jack and Williams, Mike
CULTIVATING A GENEROUS CHURCH
How To Inspire Congregational Generosity and Increase Weekly
Offerings

Jack Eason and Mike Williams, 1st ed.

Printed in the United States of America

DEDICATIONS OFFER INSIGHT

We dedicate this book to the wonderful pastors, staff, and church leaders who give their lives and their talents to inspire others.

Special thanks to Paul Pickern of www.AllProPastors.org for inspiring our decision to create this material. We are inspired by your desire to equip pastors to better serve the kingdom of God.

Special thanks to our wives and children who deal with our insane schedules so that we can help improve the financial resources of the church and para-church.

Special thanks to the Renovate Publishing Group for their diligence in bringing this material to pastors.

Special thanks to Tom Cheyney and Mark Weible for seeing the value of this material in cultivating church financial growth and creating the next generation of systematic financial partners.

A very special thanks to you the reader. May you be very blessed. We can't wait to hear your testimonies.

CONTENTS

Foreword

Mike Williams and Jack Eason are two of the funniest ministers I know! Within these pages you will discover the keys to increasing your churches weekly offering while learning from the humor and wisdom of these authors. This book is for the pastors, staff, and church leaders who give their lives and their talents every day in order to renovate their church, disciple their parishioners, and transform the world for the Lord Jesus. Pastors and churches minister in the climate where all of us are pushed, pressed and perplexed with limited attention spans. This book will help you learn how to challenge your membership to make the sacrificial commitments to support the work of ministry going on in your church. If you read the entire book and practice the sage advice within, it will undoubtedly increase your offering numbers. Try these axioms and prove to yourself that a blessing will come. These authors have used these simple fundraising axioms to raise millions of dollars every year for the local church and para-church projects. Don't miss the section on developing partnerships with those who want to support what you are doing in the community in which you minister. Learn how to speak the language so that supporters will gladly give to the ministry. The chapter on how tithing has died in so many churches is a must ready for the leader desiring to grow his church.

This book is about raising the resources necessary to further the ongoing of the work and ministry in your church. These men have helped churches and para-church organizations all over North America to develop sound methods for raising the monies that can advance the ministry. This book will leave you laughing one moment and crying the next as we work to advance the work of the Lord. Every pastor ought to read this book and invite these men in to help work in this area of stewardship. These men are walking testimonies that the Lord loves a cheerful giver and that he can use a Christian comedian and a fundraising humorist to help us learn how to present our needs before groups and individuals in such a way that is refreshing and awe inspiring. You will love these men and their humorous and encouraging spirits. Bring them to your church to help you. Allow them to challenge your membership to make the commitment to be all in for the work that God is doing in your church. Your will be glad you did.

Dr. Tom Cheyney, Founder & Directional Leader
The Renovate Group & The Renovate National
Church Revitalization Conferences

CHAPTER ONE
A Synopsis

In a world of limited time and even more limited attention spans we offer this Synopsis. Hopefully it will stir in you the desire to read the entire book, as that will undoubtedly increase your offering numbers. Try these axioms and prove to yourself that increases will come from it. Your authors use these strategic fundraising axioms to raise millions of dollars for church and para-church projects every year.

A Brain Is A Beautiful Machine

When presented the opportunity to tithe, give in an offering, or support a project, subconscious decisions are made. Often those decisions are processed in seconds. Is this project a good work? Is the presenter trustworthy? Have the planners thought through everything needed to make this project a success? Will my gift matter? How do I feel about giving to this project? How will my partnership make me feel after the check is signed? Will I be appreciated for my support tomorrow?

Not A Replacement Tithe-ology

This book does not negate tithing or systematic giving. We believe in the Biblical call to tithe, invest, share, offer, and reciprocate financially. This book will teach you how to inspire your congregation to give more generously, by understanding how God set up the human mind to receive and process information.

When you comprehend these underlying principles, you will see your tithe and offering numbers increase.

Welcome to Graceland

A boy wanted a new bicycle. His mom told him to pray and ask Jesus to bring him a bicycle for Christmas only 6 months away. The next day the young man road a new bicycle to school. His best friend wanted to know what prayer he used to get a new bicycle that quickly. He told his friend. "I didn't pray. I ripped-off the bicycle from Walmart. You could pray for 6 months and still never receive a bike. But I remember my pastor saying that God would forgive whatever we've done in an instant if I just prayed. I took the *pray-n-ride* option."

Welcome to our current generational theology. Some wonder if there can be any laws or commandments in an age of absolute glorious grace. How can a church make a case for tithing without sounding legalistic?

Here you will find seven keys every church can use to increase their tithe amounts and instill in the congregation a purpose for giving and a desire to be a significant part of that giving. The keys here are valid whether you offer plate passing, use door boxes, or operate electronic giving kiosks.

Translational Key

People are changing rapidly and the way we communicate will have to change with them. If we desire to see greater amounts of dollars in the offering, and greater amounts of people committing to systematic giving, we are going to have to invite them to be a part of our [giving] world in their [giving] language.

Our online dictionaries tell the reader that a *tithe* is something from the past. It is currently defined as *one-tenth of annual produce or earnings, formerly taken as a tax for the support of the Church and clergy.* Recent surveys have shown that 80% of college students cannot give you a definition of the *tithe* word. We are in a different culture than we were just six years ago. People are changing rapidly and the way we communicate will have to change with them.

If we desire to see greater dollar amounts in the offering, and greater amounts of systematic financial partners, we are going to have to invite participation in the language of the culture.

We inhabit a world where people have been hurt by "name it - claim it" offering narratives on one hand, and televangelist style hustlers on the other. It would behoove us to consider adding to our tithe narrative words that would make a greater connection to the current culture. Consider using "strategic partner," "shareholding partner," or "intentional investor" in your offering narratives. Speak to your congregation in words that are fresh and engaging.

Celebrational Key

Does your offering time invoke joy or boredom in the audience? Does the Deacon of the Week give a prayer of "Especially bless those who can't give..." or prayers of gratitude for our God-given ability to be

shareholders in the successful work of the church?
Does the generationally dated music we play during
the offering times declare to the younger generation
this time is not for them? Do we find ourselves
needing to host a mini-tithe sermon before every plate
passing?

Your offering time needs to be a highlight in the
service. It needs to be celebrated for what it is... a time
of planting with full knowledge that God himself will
bless the gift and the giver.

Change things up. Sing while you pass the plates.
Come forward to fill buckets as a family. Hold your
offering in your hand up to the Lord and dedicate it to
the ministry of God through the church. Even if you
are totally electronic, find a way to celebrate the joy of
giving.

Inspirational Key

People don't give because you have a need, they
give because you meet a need and they want to *be and
feel* a strategic part of that success. Everyone desires to
be a hero. We must inspire our congregation to give
with purpose, as they no longer have an appetite for
legalistic compulsion. The days of expectation is long
past us.

Armed with our multiple five forty-five-second
Inspirational stories, we must inspire people to
greatness in their systematic partnership with the
church. We must narrate encouragement through
testimonials of the success of their last gift. Inspiration
pays off.

We must continually thank them for their partnership with the finances. You can never over-thank a giver.

Preperational Key

Stop rushing the offering. We set up for the salvation invitation. An offering is an invitation to give. Stop rushing the offering preparation. Let them know the needs and what it takes to meet those needs, then encourage them to ask God for inspiration in their giving. Give them time to thank God for their own blessings and consider how they can bless God with their own giving. Give the partner time to write a check. Give them time to ask God for inspiration in their giving.

Offering preparation should come at least one song before the plates are passed. Even if your church is set up for kiosk and text giving, time is still needed to prepare the heart to give. Rushing through our giving subliminally tells our people that we are embarrassed by this biblical part of our faith.

Continuational Key

A single one-time narrative will not change the mind any more than a single reading of John 3:16 is all a person would need to read for the rest of their life. Repetition is a good teacher. However, repetition that does not appear repetitious is an *amazing* teacher.

Connect with your congregation multiple times a week through your easy to use electronics. Prep them for Sunday through your Friday and Saturday electronic connection narratives. Remind them to come prepared to give through your stories of encouragement and ministry success. Wake them on Sunday morning with a text and a smile letting them know that you are at the church and anxiously expecting their smile.

We are in a culture of tribe and connection. People are more concerned about their electronic image than anything else. Some would rather tweet a photo of being someplace special than actually being someplace special. Make the church the socially perfect place to be on Sunday. Make systematic giving partnerships the norm. Electronic peer connection and interaction drives our culture. We must use it powerfully.

Transactional Key

Are you set up to receive from our culture? Note that I did not say this generation. This entire culture is electronic, young and old. Maybe not you, but others are. To have no way to receive monetary gifts electronically in this culture is a sin. It is letting good gifts walk out the door.

Becoming electronic does not mean you abandon the offering plate or the door box. The plate will always deliver from those few who are not electronic, from those who are not yet a part of the systematic giving partnership, and from those who get paid on an irregular basis. They also offer a wonderful time of remembrance. Some churches now pass iPad along with offering plates for convenience. Let's not bring frustration to our shareholding partners by not having the ability to give through credit or debit card.

Validational Key

Be worth supporting. Be worth the cost of your operation. All the other keys combined will not overcome failing success stories. Shepherd the church to success in ministry and see the hand of God on your finances. Many of our congregation have dropped tithing because they have observed waste in the budget. They have watched or participated in budget padding. Demonstrate to the congregation your staff's frugality in daily operation while you show them your extravagance in the successful declaration of the gospel.

No Magic Wand

This not a magic formula, nor is it manipulation. If you wanted to have a good dinner you would prepare by setting the table. If you wanted to go on a long journey you would prepare by packing the suitcase with the supplies you need. You might even fill the car with gas and update your GPS before you started down the road. The keys expressed here are [intelligent] preparation from some well-worn travelers. You can prepare to receive and see greater success.

CHAPTER TWO
WHAT IS GOING ON HERE?

Stop shooting yourself in the foot! Your foot can't take another hole! Having successfully operated on underperforming offerings for the past few decades, we can tell you most church financial wounds have been self-inflicted. Former leaders have inflicted many of the wounds. But more often than not, the gun is still smoking in our well-intentioned hand as well.

When Jesus saw him lying there and learned that he had been in this condition for a long time, he asked him, "Do you want to get well?"
-John 5:6

This is "NOT" another system. It is simple wisdom... donor understanding... insider knowledge... that when considered within your repeated Sunday tithe and offering scenarios, or your special fundraisers, will radically improve your bottom line.

Scripture Matters

"I the Lord do not change. So you, the descendants of Jacob, are not destroyed. Ever since the time of your ancestors you have turned away from my decrees and have not kept them. Return to me, and I will return to you," says the Lord Almighty. "But you ask, 'How are we to return?' "Will a mere mortal rob God? Yet you rob me. "But you ask, 'How are we robbing you?' "In tithes and offerings. You are under a curse—your

8

whole nation—because you are robbing me. Bring the whole tithe into the storehouse, that there may be food in my house. Test me in this," says the Lord Almighty, "and see if I will not throw open the floodgates of heaven and pour out so much blessing that there will not be room enough to store it. I will prevent pests from devouring your crops, and the vines in your fields will not drop their fruit before it is ripe," says the Lord Almighty. "Then all the nations will call you blessed, for yours will be a delightful land," says the Lord Almighty. -Malachi 3:6-12

"You are careful to tithe even the tiniest income from your herb gardens, but you ignore the more important aspects of the law—justice, mercy, and faith. Yes, you should tithe, but do not neglect the more important things"
-Matthew 23:23/Luke 11:42 para

Consider this: whoever sows sparingly will also reap sparingly, and whoever sows bountifully will also reap bountifully. Each must do as already determined, without sadness or compulsion, for God loves a cheerful giver. Moreover, God is able to make every grace abundant for you, so that in all things, always having all you need, you may have an abundance for every good work. As it is written: "He scatters abroad, he gives to the poor; his righteousness endures forever." The one who supplies seed to the sower and bread for food will supply and multiply your seed and increase the

harvest of your righteousness.
-2 Corinthians 9:5-10 para

Some churches have grown afraid to ask for money publicly. Solutions are not found in burying the offering plate or burning the new ATM kiosks. Few people quit going to the theater because they ask for an outrageous ticket price at the door. In fact, people will spend twenty dollars on two drinks and a small popcorn without question or complaint if the movie is good.

If talking about money bothers you, you are not going to like Jesus. A significant percentage of His parables used money and possessions as their theme. If you don't want money talk, find a cheaper religion!

This book is a collection of articles and insight written by Mike G. Williams and Jack Eason to equip pastors to cultivate generosity in their people and to increase their weekly tithes and offering numbers. Together these articles expose the income generating infrastructure and narratives behind virtually every successfully funded ministry. If you need higher operating capital, this is an excellent place to start. Each article will conclude with a few questions. Your ability to implement these truths and experience the blessings are in direct correlation to your willingness to ask and answer the hard questions.

CHAPTER THREE
How Tithing Died

Yes, tithing as a norm, has died. Nevertheless, the good news is that our particular Christian faith has been specializing in resurrections for the last two thousand years!

Once upon a time in our not so distant past, Christian people tithed ten percent of the family income (net or gross) to their local church without question. There was no need for hype and narrative. It was not only expected; it was the biblical thing to do. It was so automatic and mechanized that the collection times morphed to the dullest part of the weekly gatherings. And why not? There is no need to celebrate habit.

These tithing Christians gave faithfully to their chosen denominations. These faith-keeping organizations had built our great hospitals and the places of higher theological education. They operated most of the programs for social transformation around the entire world. It is hard to be cynical about work like that!

The rise of televised religion brought many new hands reaching into the wallets of the donor pool. This new electronic church offered great music whose volume level could be controlled by the listener and polished speaking skills that always encouraged and uplifted. They never dealt with personal discipline. The pews were as comfortable as the listener's home recliner - because it was the listener's home recliner. The local church attendees began dividing their tithes and offerings between their local church and their new internationally reaching television church. This electronic church compounded the issue by giving their listeners free books, DVD sets, eagle plaques, and large-print bibles as reciprocation for every donation. Many of our antenna and cable churches promised hundred-fold heavenly blessings in response to their partnership in reaching the entire globe with their so-called Gospel message. Seriously, who wouldn't want to touch the world while receiving a hundred- fold kick-back monetary blessing and authentic Chinese-made Jerusalem artifacts, all the while fulfilling the great commission?

In a knee-jerk reaction, the local church turned its mission inward. It is called income and not an utcome. Often, church finances were shifted from world charity to other in-house needs to combat the [televised] threat to the local church. On the horizon was the super mega-church that offered much of what the electronic church offered in perks, but with a more local touch. Soon it was the battle of the mega- church versus the religious reality television, and the smaller churches struggled to reach the budget for the basics.

Tragically, these dueling bulwarks of religious power both went through a crisis of followers as significant religious figures became publicly disgraced for one reason or another. Some denominations used offering money to pay legally required reparations—or under-the-table payoffs—for the sexual sins of their leaders. All of this, within the very public eye of younger generations. People were curtailing their commitments of tithing and replacing it with a habit of non-tithing. Recent statistics show that less than four percent of Americans give to any religious organization regularly. This "regular basis" does not imply that their gifts are a full tenth or more of their income.

At the same time, the champions of business were rapidly becoming the new world order of philanthropists. Christian-esque world relief was rising mightily through the private sector, while churches remodeled their sanctuaries, many bringing them up to standards just a little shy of actual contemporary. Secular musical artists and actors became the new charitable voice of activism for the third world, declaring in a musical melody that they were the world, the people, those who would make a brighter day.

And on the eighth day, God created Bono!

Through the continuing evolvement of culture itself, newcomers to the church did not arrive with a predisposition to support the church, and certainly not at a predetermined ten-percent level. The word tithe wasn't even in their vocabulary. The concept of tithing was eroding rapidly from the past generations in an age where "grace" in everything moved to the spotlight. On another front, retirement-area pastors were receiving numerous seniors retiring to their area, utilizing their church resources, yet continuing to tithe to a former church they no longer attended in another state. Somewhere amid this time, we awoke to find that everything was different than before.

"I have a feeling we're not in Kansas anymore."

- Dorothy, Wizard of Oz

Stop! Something has to be done. The church gas tanks are empty, and nobody seems to want to pay the price to fill them. Fortunately, we all possess the latest electronic gadgets. Praise God for that!

Many leaders have been studying these evolving trends. Observant leaders quickly realize their need for a new tithe narrative to speak to this multi-age, contemporary culture. Wise pastors are developing a new narrative to enlist, engage, and connect the potential donor. This is not a shift in biblical doctrine, as calling people to tithe has always been a challenge for the leadership. Instead, we are seeing a change from old words to new words and old giving scenarios to new giving scenarios in a new world mindset.

Enlightened leaders are learning to postulate their requests for funding with a Jesus style of narrative. This new narrative will motivate and create the next generation of church financial shareholders. These enlightened leaders understand this new multi-aged, post-modern culture will not give because you tell them about needs. They will only give because you meet needs successfully and they want a piece of the significance. In a world of charity overload and compassion fatigue, that becomes a huge difference.

Of course, I have a red philanthropic iPhone. I don't know what I sponsored, but I want you to know that I sponsored something. I am socially compassionate!

Today, the pastor must resist asking their congregation to give to the vagueness of "the church." Pastors and leaders must show the potential donor what the genuine needs are and show how the donor-partner, together with the church, will meet those needs. Successful fundraising pastors are finding ways to share needs rapidly, find fixes quickly, and sharing both need and solution in a captivatingly inspirational story.

Today's successful fundraising minister understands the need to build trust as if it never existed. For many of their audience, faith in religious organizations never did exist. Trust has withered away over the years, thanks to those unscrupulous pitchmen and the nationally televised corruption. This successful leader works to restore trust and community before he considers his church worthy of generous and systematic giving.

This leader works to build community because community meets funds itself. Inside the church walls, successful offering scenarios will reject the somber, almost depressing mode of the traditional offering moments (circa-1960), featuring a pianist playing unfamiliar melodies that isolate the younger audience. These successful leaders are returning to a biblical stance of giving with a cheerful, hilarious heart in a time of celebration and happiness. Giving is becoming joyfully celebrated during a strategic part of every service, often with clapping of hands to the most exceptional, most uplifting music of the day.

In a world of high competition from para-church organizations and electronic churches, it is easy to become the invisible local steeple. Successful pastor-fundraisers must move from the lethargic expectations of a ten-percent offering plate, received in a single, rounded plate or wooden wall-mounted box. They must diversify their collection mechanisms. They must utilize advanced electronic options of donating to meet the need in this rapidly transforming, cashless society. They must choose to engage and impassion their audience with a clear understanding of the amounts needed to change the need situation into a success story. These leaders know how to articulate gratitude for their shareholders.

Leaders who learn to respond appropriately to donor-partners with repetitive responses of thanksgiving, making the donor the hero of every project, will see an increase in donations and giving. Through this, the donor-partner gains personal and spiritual significance, which is a core desire behind any gift. This personal significance gives the donor an increased desire to give again.

Success must be among the voices that congregations hear from their leaders in every morning's social media posts. These leaders are not taking their donors' trust for granted. They rapidly provide proof of the project's completion. When the proof is given, success is celebrated! Each time a project is brought to fulfillment, we can ask again and receive again.

Long-term success becomes the norm for the leaders who infuse the narrative partnership principles into every aspect of their church or Christian organization, reinforcing the principles into their everyday teaching narratives. They systematically insert an underlying stewardship message, which lies beneath the surface of every sermon, song, class, and activity they allow.

Language Changes

In this culture of new verbiage, the old English word tithe has fallen by the wayside, along with his brothers: propitiation, furlong, gainsay, husbandman, untoward, twain, and verily-verily. However, they are still faithfully taught by successful leaders who care more about the meaning behind the word than about whatever the pronunciation of the word is that day.

All this sounds like a colossal chore, undoable, or exhausting. The truth is that it as easy making scrambled eggs when you get the hang of it. It will come as second nature when you get it in your soul. But even if it does take work, hard work, it is worth it.

The next few articles will give you easy and creative techniques (insight) for monetary appeals. They will enlighten you to a new giving narrative that will result in a fully funded church by a larger congregation of financial partners who are taking the church to a new level of work for the kingdom of God. Many souls will be transformed, and many hungry countries will be fed. *And we might humorously hope that all the enlightened pastors and leaders received annual raises every year until they retired in Florida on a great pension.*

Though the opening declarations are articulated in a language designed for the local church, the principles are not limited to the local church. These same principles are being used successfully by mission organizations, missionaries, Christian schools, hospitals, and faith-based radio stations across the country.

Along with material written exclusively for this publication, this book contains topical articles we (Mike G. Williams / Jack Eason) have written for the Workshops we have hosted around the country. Many of the articles have interwoven themes. Excellent, as repetition is the best teacher. Welcome to the conversation.

QUESTIONS TO PONDER:

1. What comment from this section immediately jumped out at you?
2. If you read nothing else in the book, what are you now thinking about changing in your offering-tithing narrative?

CHAPTER FOUR
ARTICLE - What Language is That?

Perhaps the struggle to get the church members and attendees off their wallets has been going on longer than we might have thought. I'm sure that our Old Testament leaders had a few cheapskates and naysayers. Thus, every generation of clergy has found a new, culturally compelling narrative to reach God's stingy, albeit chosen few.

From this church field they said you are moving, We will not shed a tear when you go, Because you said that we all should be tithers, And offended the membership so.
Last Sunday you preached about tithing. And you made eye contact with me, And from that point until now I've been angry, Because I'm saved by grace which was free.
-unknown

Hair Club for Men

We are closely watching the hair replacement commercials offering their real, transplanted, and artificial turf to the folic-challenged consumer for physical implantation or re-implantation into their head. Honestly, the whole process sounds a little strange from the get-go. Nevertheless, if you can remove a heart from a pig and place it in a man, who are we to judge what can be done with simple hair? If you looked at either of your authors, you might think our interest to be personal. Although today we each have a reasonably good handful of follicles on the cranium, we are seeing more vanish every day.

There is a more significant reason we are studying hair implant commercials. We are watching an ever-changing personal grooming trend. Our current culture does not seem as entranced with keeping their head covered with hair. They seem to glory in removing the scalp hair, polishing it like a bowling ball, and feverishly growing their chin hair. In an age where we are so afraid of Muslim extremist brothers, post-modernity is doing everything it can to look like them. Maybe we should blame our dear Christian brethren, affectionately known as *Duck Dynasty*. Perhaps not. How will these hair businesses continue to thrive? Will they continue to pitch the same old pitch, or will they be able to create a return-to-hair trend and save their scalps in the process? Pardon the pun. The hair transplant business is right where many readers are, both hair-wise and trend-wise.

Let's start with six quick questions. Do you need to increase the amount of income your church is receiving? Would you like to meet your weekly budget? Would you like to buy some printer ink cartridges without having to call a special business meeting to approve the purchase? Would you like for people to give generously and automatically? Would you like to see the senior winter visitors giving to their wintertime church? Would you like to see younger people get involved in tithes and offerings? Would you like to know the secrets that the hugely successful para-church organizations are using to garner large quantities of money?

Before we go too far into this discussion, we need to make full disclosure. Both of your authors are ordained pastors, active in local churches, and are responsible for the fundraising for a mid-sized mission in a developing country. We've both written numerous books and have made our living helping non-profits garner more substantial gifts from donors. Our business expertise and success has thrust us into the middle of a vast world of major non-profit organizations. We are helping those non-profits raise millions of dollars, and in turn, they help us fund our international mission projects. There are plenty of donors and money out there. Our objective is to help you receive a fair share ... and, of course, use that for the cause of the good Gospel.

> *"Tithing is like training wheels when it comes to giving. It's intended to help you get started, but not recommended for the Tour de France."*
> *- John Ortberg, Author[1]*

Let's get right to it. Some might believe that learning how to ask for money seems like a rather carnal ambition. Does going to seminary to learn how to preach a better sermon seem carnal? Does learning how to speak English so you can communicate intelligently with your English listener seem unspiritual? If education in one area is wrong, if learning from experience is wrong, if using a disciple-maker or coach to help a person develop their God-given potential is wrong, then this information needs to be burned along with the rock-n-roll albums we burned after Sunday night youth group back in our

---

[1] https://www.christianitytoday.com/pastors/2013/spring/tithing-law-or-grace.html

teens. Hotel California and Desperado needed to be dealt with by fire, and so does any of our educational programs.

If you have a mind to consider that there may be a more monetary resources out there, welcome. If you think that metanoia can work in areas outside of salvation, you are pre-approved to join our discussion. We do call it an ongoing conversation, as connecting with an ever-fluid giving culture will change.

Some might feel they already know how to ask for money expertly. Pastors, like everyone else, often suffer from what psychologists term the Dunning–Kruger effect. It's a cognitive bias wherein people believe they are much better at doing something than they really are. Why is it that one fundraiser will make a financial ask and receive a 40-percent response and another will present to the same audience and receive a 95-percent response? Let us agree that we can all get better at doing what we already know how to do.

Word Up

Can you remember the arguments over the KJV and the NKJV Bible years ago? Those discussions were not over the authority of the Bible or its authenticity. Those discussions, otherwise known as arguments, took place over which version of the Bible was better. Our fathers' generation believed there was only one KJV Bible. It was the Bible whose opening pages declared it to be the authorized version by King James himself.

As modern English translations surfaced, so did the ranting tirades about the "modern, heretical, liberal, hell-bound, Satan-inspired publishers" that had corrupted the Bible to such a high degree that God would certainly destroy our entire earth as He did the cities of Sodom and Gomorrah. What could be the perversion so great as to cause this? The newer versions—The New King James Bible, The New International Version, The Revised Standard Version, and even the Phillips New Testament, to name a few—had changed, modified, updated their word lexicon. Many sincerely felt that these new translations were sent in an attempt to destroy the faith. *Time will tell.*

Make no mistake, we wholeheartedly believe the sacredness of Scripture. In fact, we believe that everyone needs to hear the Word of God in their own language and at their personal reading level. *Go Wycliffe!*

Today, most of us understand that the Word of God holds the same power in any language (Spanish, English, French). Most agree the translation of the Word of God must match the audience's ability to understand it. This is where we stand today with the word tithe. Albeit a beautiful word, the tithe has been left by the wayside in our workaday world. In prepping for these workshops, we randomly interviewed twenty college students on a Methodist University campus and asked them to define tithe. Few of the guys had heard the word. Only three of the girls knew it to be attached to giving to a church. Two of those three knew it meant giving ten percent of your income after taxes. For the record, the word stewardship scored very low on the cognitive recognition scale as well.

Tithing is considerably less inspirational than words like systematic partnership or shareholding member.

We adapt almost everything in the church to fit the culture. Our buildings rival that of current modern architecture. Our restrooms have become practically useable, thank the Lord. Our church sound systems now match the rock shows of ten years past. Many of us grew up in a church where drums were considered the instrument that gained Satan expulsion from heaven. Today there is rarely a church that does not have them. Some consider these changes as liberal, while others define it as relevant.

Our straight-backed, hard, oak, repentance-producing pews have been replaced by comfortable padded chairs. The old wooden floors that would groan as you walked them have been replaced by new carpet. Beautiful stained-glass windows and natural sunlight have been replaced by window shades and intelligent lighting systems that rival Disney World productions. No longer do the seniors consider the lighting systems as better left in a disco. Our current senior generation were the ones who attended Woodstock and loved it. *They have the tattoos to prove it.*

Even the modern Plexiglas podiums (circa-1980) have been declared vintage. Our church no longer has a podium, formerly known as a pulpit (word change). It has been replaced by a round Starbucks coffee-esque high-top table to create an open and sharing environment. *Coffee anyone?*

More to Come

Let us go a little further. Sunday church used to mean 9:30 a.m. Sunday School, followed by 11:00 a.m. worship. In the afternoon, the youth group (now referred to as student ministry) went out to lead services at the nursing home (now referred to as the Senior Living Apartments and Memory Care Center). We would all be back to the church by 6:00 p.m. for Training Union (now morphed into home groups or small groups, if we even have them). At 7:00 p.m., we had evening worship for another hour or more (now referred to as "discontinued due to lack of interest"). After evening worship, we headed to Denny's or Dairy Queen to fellowship with the people we spent most of the day with. That was our Sunday. It was the Lord's day, and He, or at least His people, got most of it. It was not a task; it was the norm.

But wait, there was more. We had a Wednesday night prayer meeting, followed by choir practice (now called worship band rehearsal). On Thursday nights, the committed believers met to go out on church visitation. The sick and the afflicted (another phrase that has been replaced), those in the hospital, and anyone who visited the church received a [drop-by their house] personal visit. If there were no sick or visitors, we would often take a block in our neighborhood and visit door to door (a phrase and action replaced by social media campaigns). We could go on, but we won't.

We are a church, a people, a country of metanoia. Change is in our blood. We have hopefully kept the good Gospel of Jesus (though some might question that) while translating the Gospel and our approach to it into words and actions our culture understands. We [have] tried—with fervency—to be culturally relevant in many areas. Nevertheless, there is the tithe issue!

"The Gospels were written to present the life and teachings of Jesus in ways that would be appropriate to different readerships, and for that reason are not all the same. They were not intended to be biographies of Jesus, but selective accounts that would demonstrate his significance for different cultures."
-John Drane, Theologian[2]

We welcome an objection here. Some of you might be saying that your church is filled with people who are not offended by the word tithe. Maybe you are in a church that is not expanding with conversion growth. Maybe you pastor a senior saints church. Praise God. We need those too. A dear friend in South Florida cheerfully and jokingly proclaims, "At First Church of the Rapidly Departing, the average age of my congregation is deceased. But they continue to give well." *He is not having a tithing crisis; he is having a funeral crisis. His old faithful people are rapidly moving on to cash in their heavenly investments.* He is a few years away from a financial crisis. Many pastors suffer with a group of transplanted, retired snowbird parishioners continuing to tithe to their former church, even though they are now absorbing the resources of their new church. This demographic needs to be re- trained. Staying a senior

---

2 https://zondervanacademic.com/blog/gospel-definition

church might work in some retirement areas, but if the old churches do not receive new blood into the church, all of their past tithes will eventually become a strip mall or medical center. Every church needs to invest in its future leadership.

"If all Christians and Jews tithed their income as the Bible commands, every poor person would be cared for, every naked person clothed, and every hungry person fed."
—Ann Coulter, Author, Political activist[3]

View the following opinion condensed from a number of conversations, preparing for this article:

"Why should I tithe? The tithe was set up to take care of the priests, maintain the church building, feed hungry people, care for the widows, house the orphans, and serve the sick. The church does not do that anymore. They should be able to run the place on a lot less now that the government is doing most of their social work. I consider my taxes to be part of my tithe. Maybe the tithes should be reduced to like, two percent, instead of ten. That is just my opinion. I'm Evangelical Protestant, but I grew up Catholic. It used to be that a priest took vows of poverty. What happened to that?"

What does that testimony tell us? What observations can we make about the mindset of this

---

[3] https://www.brainyquote.com/quotes/ann_coulter_838669

potential financial partner? What would you say or demonstrate to change his mindset?

So What Now?

Let us look specifically at how to increase your church's income using tithing and unique offerings. This discussion is not about trading your round, wooden offering plates for furry red bags with two or three handles on them (an excellent 80s innovation). *If round plates were good enough for Jesus, they are good enough for us.* This discussion is not about placing credit card scanners on the rim of every offering plate, although we know of a church that passes iPads around every week with the plates. It is not about replacing your plate-passing tradition with humble, unobtrusive boxes near every exit or installing ATM kiosks near the coffee shop. Neither are we against any of those systems. We will assist you in finding culturally correct tithe and offering narratives to speak into the heart and mind of your demographic.

On Another Front

Pastors are in a battle for income share with major philanthropic organizations who are spending a large percentage of their income to generate more revenue. Profit from your people! How will you compete? Some of those reading this may be aging, tired, and in the midst of merely riding out their time to retirement, hoping the church will resurrect after they are gone. God forbid! Let's look at how we can effectively communicate the message of the tithe and offering to an ever-younger audience whose language has morphed before our eyes. "We do bequest, whilst thou joinest us thy brethren on this journey?" *Sorry, those old languages die slow.* Let us re-phrase. Are you ready to turn more people on to systematic shareholding and increase the financial bottom line of your church or para-church organization? Then shout out, "Show me the tithe money!"

> *"I absolutely believe in the power of tithing and giving back. My own experience about all the blessings I've had in my life is that the more I give away, the more that comes back. That is the way life works, and that is the way energy works."*
> **-Ken Blanchard, Author**[4]

It is not necessary that you agree with every axiom. You may not appreciate many of the illustrations or the things we find humorous. We are fine with that. However, we know that these time-tested axioms will help you, even if you only venture to use one simple axiom.

QUESTIONS TO PONDER:

1. Has your church held fast to any words that are no longer used?

---

[4] www.brainyquote.com/quotes/ken_blanchard_173323

2. What church traditions could be hindering your effectiveness in teaching tithing or any other area of ministry?

3. Do you shy away from talking about tithing?

4. If you could not use the word tithe or offering for the next 60 days, what word would you feel most comfortable using?

5. Is there a reason you could not attempt using this new word for the next 60 days?

CHAPTER FIVE
Article - Transactions Or Interactions

Read the following narratives that represent material we received while preparing for a recent tithing workshop:

"My church took me through the Dave Ramsey series and taught me to be smart with my money, to know where it was going, and to appreciate the effort involved with making it. Now the church wants me to give them ten percent of it without asking them if they are using it frugally or with the same standards that they taught. The church wants us to simply trust them. I want to know if my tithes and offerings are doing anything worth supporting. I don't think that's too much to ask from a church that gave me the training to begin with."

"There are a lot of churches with a lot of buildings and big mortgages. I want a community of believers who have something in common. As a single mother, I don't have a lot to give. I will support the church or para-church that keeps my son connected with God. That is what I am willing to support. I can hear a great sermon anywhere."

"The church across town offers my family great programming, gorgeous productions, and uplifting messages. They have an amazing program for my younger children and a gymnasium with a rock-climbing wall for my teenager. They offer services at different times, or we can watch a well-produced service on my cell phone if we can't be there on Sunday. We can even donate through the phone. I get a video devotional from their pastor on my phone every morning, and we are not even members there. Unless the church we are currently attending can show they are doing something 'Community Impacting' with my tithe money, why would I not go to a place that at least gives me great amenities for my donations?"

"I want to know that what I give will go to support the Great Commission. Whether or not I am actively engaging people in evangelism myself, I want to at a minimum believe that my money is providing church professionals who are actively engaging the community in evangelism. If the current leaders are not reaching people for Christ, how could they teach me how to do it? I want to support the work of evangelism. That is what moves me. This is why we gave faithfully to Billy Graham for so many years. He knew how to bring people to Christ."

"My church has a couple of thousand square feet of tiny little brick classrooms that are now sitting empty. Who has twenty tiny classes of six people anymore? According to our finance committee, the biggest waste of funds is the cost to climate control all of this vacant, unused space. I worked to pay for this building, and now I have to keep it cool to preserve the value of it until we undoubtedly sell it to some other church congregation who will fill it. I want to see my past tithes and present tithes be used to reach people with a Gospel message in the years I have left. Yes, I am tempted to go to my son's church. The only thing keeping me here are friends."

"I worked on staff in a church for many years. I have seen wasted money. At the end of every fiscal year, every department would rush to spend their money on anything they could to make it look as if they needed more money the next year. They wasted God's money on the hopes that they would get more to waste the next year. Can I as a good steward give to that kind of waste? Would that be the right thing to do?"

Those are some interesting and transparent testimonial statements. How would your church answer the questions and accusations that are embedded in these statements?

Let's Get A Room

Last week, we attended a conference in Washington, DC. We didn't stay at the overly expensive hotel where the conference was held. Rather, we opted for a beautiful little rental house just a short walk from the meeting. Let's see what we might be able to learn from a company known as Airbnb.com.

One of the things that most of us in the church world give little time thinking about is the amount of trust our partners, members, or attendees give to us. At the core of our relationship with our congregation is the fact that they trust us with their hard-earned money; they choose to give to our church. What does that have to do with Airbnb?

The first time we used Airbnb was several years ago, and admittedly, it took a little bravery to try it. Staying in someone else's home and treating it like you would a hotel is a little "out of the box" for most people's taste. Conversely, one could not help but wonder if pictures shown online could be trusted and if the stay would be a pleasant one. But a friend's encouragement—and of course, YELP testimonials— allowed us to trust enough to make that click for the first time.

After that first experience, Airbnb became a trusted friend. Each visit provided great experiences of meeting new, often fascinating people. The hosts have always shared unique things about their city, favorite places they eat, or sights that were a "must see" while in the area. As a result, choosing Airbnb is not a big deal anymore. After repeated pleasant interactions, a client is no longer fearful of the unknown situations they might find themselves in by booking a stay through Airbnb. Those consistently pleasant interactions have built up a foundation of trust in Airbnb.

Are you familiar with Airbnb? At the time of this writing, Airbnb is the second most valuable hospitality company in the world. It connects people in over 65,000 cities in 191 countries and has served over 200 million guests. Believe it or not, in the beginning, the founders of Airbnb were not concerned about building their company on the money. The currency that Airbnb was built upon was trust amongst people who did not know each other: the person staying as a guest in the home, apartment, or townhouse and the owner-renter of the property. The co-founders of Airbnb decided early on they didn't want to build only a marketplace, but an interactive community of friends and fans. They believed that community would build their marketplace. Most marketplaces are built on money, and most businesses are built on money, but the founders of Airbnb knew the money will only go so far. And they wanted something that would turn into a movement.

If you create a business based on money, that business will become transactional. If money is the currency of transactions, trust is the currency of interactions. Airbnb wanted to build interactions and community because they recognized that trust would build Airbnb into the hospitality organization they dreamed it could be. They also knew that increased interactions would increase profitability.

What can a church learn from Airbnb? People are being asked to make "trust leaps" more and more with technology in our culture. The first time someone used eBay was a trust leap. The first time someone had something delivered by an Amazon drone was a trust leap. The first time we used Uber was a trust leap. The reality is, these types of trust leaps are happening more frequently in society. Connecting new people to our churches—people who've had no experience with us—is an unknown for that prospective member or attendee. Trying to garner new members who have never given financially to our churches is asking them to move to the unknown. And for most people, that's a vast chasm to cross. It is a trust leap! They don't know us yet, and so they aren't going to be comfortable giving to our churches until trust has been established. There is an unknown risk. We have to understand that when we are asking people to give financially to our church, it requires a risk on their part.

The bridge that transports people from the unknown to the known is named Trust.

We cannot forget the trust bridge. It is not optional. The challenge we face is the unfortunate fact that there are a lot of places that are betraying the trust of people every day. You don't have to look too far to find a news article or a television report about social security numbers being compromised or someone's personal information being stolen. Not only that, but let's face it: many churches have breached the trust of their members and attendees. Pastors or church treasurers have embezzled money from churches. Television pastors have been documented living in multi-million-dollar homes while raising money to supposedly help the poor in their communities.

We can hit a pulpit or a high-top coffee table with our fist and shout that "Believers should tithe and support the work of the church." Unfortunately, sitting in the pews are people whose trust has been broken, breached, and violated. And they are skeptical about giving for those exact reasons. The fact is, even our current members and attendees would probably confess to us (if asked) that they sometimes wonder if their money is going to make an impact if their money is going where we say it is, or if it's just being consumed to build a consumer-driven congregation. We must give these questions some thought. Add to that the fact that many now sitting in our sanctuary at this point know very little if anything, about biblical stewardship, and we have a tough job in front of us.

You and I may know it's biblical to give, but we live in a new world where that's not a given anymore. We may not like it, but we have to face the fact that is where people are if we are going to change the mindset and culture of our congregations. So, how can we get people to trust our church with their money? Great question! Because of our culture and the lack of trust in our world, people expect certain things from our church and, perhaps, even demand them. Here are a few expectations:

Responsiveness

When someone engages with our church, they expect a speedy response. We live in a society where people expect instant gratification. Our responsiveness will dictate the level of trust that current and future members and attendees have with us. If we are slow to respond, they will question our ministry and begin to doubt our effectiveness. We must understand how they feel. As those who serve non-profits, even some of the ministries we consult are slow to get back to us through email or phone. Today, we as church leaders seem nearly impossible to reach. We have so many layers of "protection" from our church members; it's as if the Secret Service is protecting our church leaders. *And Elvis seems to have always quietly left the building.*

If you are unresponsive or unapproachable, you are going to have difficulty building trust with your people. Unfortunately, like politics, our congregation knows the best way to get an audience with the pastor is through a significant gift. It works for me.

Our responsiveness is important. It gives a good impression—sometimes the first impression—to those who are trying to reach out and connect with us. Even social media platforms are rating profiles based on the responsiveness of the profile owner. The speed at which we answer gives us a better rating in that platform. According to J.D. Power, 67% of consumers have used a company's social media channel for customer service.[5] And when they do, they expect a fast response. Research cited by Jay Baer tells us that 42% of consumers expect a response within sixty minutes.[6] We must be willing to connect with people. Ministry is people.

Ownership

Our church members want to be seen, at a minimum, as shareholders and prefer to be owners of the ministry they support. Don't fear. That's a good thing. When they feel ownership, they are more

---

5 www.jdpower.com/business/.../2013-social-media-benchmark-study

6 https://www.convinceandconvert.com/social-media-research/42-percent-of-consumers-complaining-in-social-media-expect-60-minute-response-time/

involved and more committed to the mission of the church. If you don't see your members as owners in the ministry, then you aren't seeing them as they want to be seen. Hopefully, you would never treat a co-owner of your business like you don't have time for them. If they are a co-owner, their input and interaction is seen as invaluable. That's the way our church members want to be seen today. Because trust has been breached by so many organizations in the past, most church members aren't going to be content to give you money and have no interaction. We have to find ways to incorporate their financial partnership, with the option of participation.

Accountability

Effective communication with our members tells them we are accountable to them. What kind of effective communication do you share with your members and attendees? Do you have "closed-door" meetings for only a few, or are you transparent with the financial details of the church? It would do all of us good to be reminded that as each additional person gives money to our church, we add yet another person to the list to whom we are accountable. We, as leaders, answer to each person whose financial resources have made it possible to accomplish our mission. To the post-modern culture, this is a biggie. If you can't show accountability, it doesn't matter what ministry is being accomplished, you will not receive the greatest possible success.

Accountability includes showing what the ministry is accomplishing. We've voiced this in previous articles on the subject, but it bears repeating. If you can't give a visual, testimonial, or statistical data for the impact of your ministry, people are going to be less apt to give. The reality is that most of us are getting bombarded by email and snail mail with organizations asking for money. The ones that are receiving the finances are the ones who can effectively tell about the impact of their ministry. Remember, it's not the one that is doing the most ministry that gets the funding. It's the ministry that does the best job [communicating] the ministry that sees the green. And they are doing it in a way that shows accountability.

> *"Non-profit leaders tend to pay attention to accountability once a problem of trust arises."*
> *Alnoor Ebrahim, Harvard Business School[7]*

Let's be honest. Stuff happens. Financial mistakes happen to the best of us. *The time to be honest and open is long before the omnishambles.* The time to create trust is in good times, so when the problem happens, there has been a history of openness and accountability. Then your partners, your co-owners, will bear the brunt of the storm with you and not turn it against you. Don't wait until something happens to be accountable to the membership, even the non-member contributors.

---

[7] www.hbs.edu/faculty/publication%20files/10-069.pdf

Empathy

People don't care how much you know until they know how much you care. A missionary friend helps prepare short-term mission visitors for developing world ministry by instructing them how to relate to the people they will be talking with. She says, "People do not connect with you by hearing about your trophies. These poor people have no trophies. They will connect with you by hearing about your scars. They have many scars of their own."

Failed church ministry investments have wounded your current and potential financial partners. Can you feel for them? Are you addressing that or pushing it under the rug? We must develop true and genuine empathy for our partners, our shareholders, our donors, our tithers, our co-owners, and even our mere observers, who have been broken by failures of leadership in our church denominations and para-church ministries.

"While sympathy is compassion for someone else's situation, empathy is feeling their pain." Mary Cahalane, Fundraising Developer[8]

Because most people in society have had their trust breached by some organization at one time or another, we must empathize with our members and givers in this regard. Any additional steps we can take

---

[8] www.hbs.edu/faculty/publication%20files/10-069.pdf

to show we empathy with them will be helpful at gaining and keeping their trust. Sharing financial information (when appropriate), providing timely updates on giving, sharing proof of project - mission completion, and becoming a part of financial accountability groups all tell our members we empathize with them and understand their trust is a sacred partnership. And we are willing to make it a priority to prove to them that they are worthy of our understanding and transparency.

QUESTIONS TO PONDER:

1. How rapidly responsive is your organization when someone connects with you online?
2. Do you check your website links every week to assure they are working correctly?
3. Do your partners feel like they are co-owners of your organization? Why or why not?
4. How do you express empathy with your partners?
5. What are some ways you demonstrate accountability to your partners?

CHAPTER SIX
ARTICLE - Become Bi-lingual

Unless we understand the secret motivational language of our congregation (our clients), we will not be able to speak to them in their heart language. Our goal is that you will fully understand how to speak in the narrative (language) and secondary narrative (N2) of your listener.

In Acts, we are told that the crowd was amazed because each one heard in their own [cultural/native] language. If the Spirit of God speaks in the cultural language of the listener, should we not attempt to do the same?

The changes we see before our eyes are not a matter of Builders becoming Boomers, who become Busters, who become... and so on and so on. The congregants of our world and church are somewhat fluid. Each generation becomes more everything, even as the generation behind it becomes more blasé or tolerant or even more liberal versus conservative. We refuse to lock your current audience into identification groups such as Buster or Millennial or X, or Y, or Z. We would rather consider that each group moves fluidly forward in a culture of now. Many of the senior saints we deal with are as post-modern as the twenties demographic, just a little more hindered by arthritis. Each age has changed within their selves. So, post-modern, though mentioned heavily in our discussions, is not an age group. It is a culture.

A Hitch In The Plan

We are in the midst of a "grace revolution." We understand we are saved by grace through faith, no good works involved. It is all God's grace through Jesus. You know what we are talking about. We are not playing it up or down.

Question: In the mind of the grace generation, has tithing-giving become an option or suggestion? Some believe that this post-modern generation, as we see its current apparition, as going back to the 1980s. For some, leaving out the need for tithing is an effort to become more inviting. For others, it was a desire to fully appreciate a Gospel that did not subliminally call good works (tithing) into the salvation process. Either way, the grace generation is here.

"What a waste to attempt to change behavior without truly understanding the driving needs that cause such behavior."
-Robert S. McGee, The Search for Significance[9]

Do you remember when drinking wine or beer or cocktails, consuming tobacco products *(unless you were a deacon)*, using profane language, lotteries, visiting a casino, going to an eatery that served booze, and even going to Hollywood-made movies were considered way outside the lifestyle of the true Christian believer? Did your church have a written or unwritten list of standards in your formative years? We will bet that

---

9 www.justfaithalone.com/downloads/2013/03/searchforsignifi00mcge.pdf

under your leadership, there are a lot more acceptable practices than there were under your childhood pastor's leadership. Are we correct? It was only a few years ago that divorce placed a scarlet letter upon your ability to serve in any church capacity. Times have changed.

In some parts of the country, unless a pastor has a shaved head, a beard, and makes craft beer in his basement, he is considered out of touch with the Christian society. Again, we are not here to justify or condemn that. We are proving the culture of change. *Party on Pastor Wayne. Party on Pastor Garth.* To some in this fluid grace generation, you are out of touch if you don't include an expletive or at least allude to one in your sermon, if to only prove your humanity as a leader.

> **"True, tithing is a grace issue. So now we have the opportunity to give twenty percent, thirty percent, or even more to the work of God's Kingdom."**
> **-Andy Stanley**[10]

The current grace belief lingers into... if the same laws that prohibited us from eating pork and lobster were done away with, then tithing, which came within the same Old Testament era, must have been done away with too. And if not, who cares? We live under grace; forgiveness is a prayer away. God loves me because I am a beautiful person on the inside.

---

[10] https://briandoddonleadership.com/2016/06/12/42-quotes-and-lessons-from-andy-stanley-on-money-and-possessions/

Motion Everywhere

As the major companies have changed from employee loyalty to stockholder loyalty, this fluid generation has lost much of its lifelong brand loyalty. What is really real anymore? Often, faux branded products are sold to us as real. Even on Amazon! *If you watch 20/20, you already know this.*

This fluid generation's political and educational leaders have proven themselves to be less than altruistic, and even their religious leaders, who in previous generations stood before them Sunday mornings on end, now swap out every other Sunday with a co-pastor. They are very used to multiple and changing voices. The devout believer in this fluid generation has thousands of additional podcast pastors available to them at any time, on any schedule, at any convenience. This generation is not limited to the scheduled singular Sunday morning service or radio broadcast.

Go back to our first chapter and re-read the story of the boy with the stolen bicycle. This story, to a large extent, represents the mindset of many combination modern-postmodern-Evangelical-Protestant- grace loving congregations. We might even go as far as to include the mindset of deacons, elders, support staff, and, of course, the student ministers in our painting. Sure, there are some exceptions, but we are merely using a broad brush here.

Generations Morph

Some try to define groups like Builders, Busters, Boomers, Millennials, X, Y, Z, and Post-modernists with a surgeon's scalpel-like precision. It can't be done. Each generation or demographic takes on the disposition of the future generation as they get older. One might question which came first, the chicken or the egg. Maybe the actions of the next generation are the reactions to the previous generation. Is it nature, nurture, increasing entropy, education, liberal influences, or something deeper?

You cannot make a Mason-Dixon Line between age groups. Some people don't fit in either category. Depending upon your social status, political party, religious practice, and so much more, you may have found yourself in the described mindset of the Builders, Busters, Boomers, Millennials, X, Y, Z, and Post-modernists simultaneously.

We all move to a more contemporary position in our thinking as the calendar goes forward. We don't use the Baptist hymnal from 1971 anymore, as many use the brand new 1995 hymnal. Some have video screens in their church. Some pastors, even those of senior age, preach from an iPad. Some believe those will have to stand before God one day for bringing technology into the church, amen.

Does your church have a contemporary service or traditional? Which circa is your traditional service? Early church? The 1800s? How about 1957? *It was a classic year for cars and hymnals.* What circa is your contemporary service? The 80s, 90s, 2000, 2010? How many churches are using music dropped from the latest (modern) Skillet CD or Bethel MP3 as their go-to music for Sunday morning? Musical styles morph the traditional lines too. Daring to call our circa-1960 services "traditional" has always been considered a farce by our Easter Orthodox brethren whose traditional services more closely emulate that of circa 300 A.D. We have all chosen a (date) culture to maintain as traditional. Understanding that, we must not become judgmental or critical without first applying those judgments to ourselves.

"A rich man without charity is a rogue; and perhaps it would be no difficult matter to prove that he is also a fool." - Henry Fielding, Novelist[11]

It's a Tower of Babel out there. Have you noticed that even our everyday language has morphed? Words are pronounced differently now than when we were children.

**"I'm not too old to learn a new language."
- C.T. Studd, at 50 years of age, Missionary to China, India, Africa**[12]

Tell us the last time you heard [tithe] used outside of church? We know where our pronunciation of the word comes from—the old English, of course. The same ancient generations that gave us the Great Bible, the Geneva Bible, and the King James Authorized Version Bible (affectionately mentioned earlier). *Please*

---

11 https://www.quotes.net/quote/44476
12 www.goodreads.com/author/quotes/3441241.C_T_Studd

pardon our blatant omission of John Wycliffe, William Tyndale, Myles Coverdale, and many more deserving respectful nods.

When teaching this material as a workshop, we often bring out huge flash cards and play a little game with old words. There are so many words that have left our ancient English vernacular in the past fifty years. *That might include the word vernacular.*

On the other hand, we have new words that didn't exist twenty years ago. Google, blog, mashup, bromance, cyberstalking, omnishambles, staycation, sexting, upcycle, metrosexual, locavore, and hater was not part of our last generation's lexicon. Hater is one that is often used in conjunction with religion, so we know you have been made aware of that one. Locavore has hit the scene lately. It is the choice to eat only food grown within 250 miles of your location. You'd better only do that if you also choose an eco-friendly staycation. The splendid word omnishambles became the Word of the Year in the Oxford Dictionary only a short time back. *We were not invited to the ceremony, were you?*

After much discussion, debate, and certainly in-depth research, *post-truth* became Oxford Dictionary's Word of the Year for 2016. It's an adjective defined as "relating to or denoting circumstances in which objective facts are less influential in shaping public opinion that appeals to emotion and personal belief." *We find that word very intriguing in this generation and appropriate for this culture.* Need we say more?

Understandable Language

You need to speak the dialect of your audience.

You need to consider if the tithe is even understood by your listeners. You also need to consider if that word brings up good emotions or bad feelings. If we are willing to remove the denominational branding (Baptist, Southern Baptist, Assembly of God, Presbyterian, COG, AME) from our signs to disassociate with people's past negative experiences with our denominations, why would we not be willing to use a more common word to replace the phrase tithe or tithing? *That question is not rhetorical.*

Before any of us fight to canonize the English pronunciation of the tithe word, let us consider bringing back other words like propitiation and begotten to the table too. If we have to explain their meaning anyway, let's use the words we would use to tell them in the first place. Why clutter Biblical truth? Compare how often Jesus quoted from the Torah to how many culturally relevant parables He delivered. Jesus spoke the cultural language of his *Torah loving* culture.

Consider a few suggestions for our post-modern tithe narratives:

Great Commission Shareholder

Systematic Shareholder

Partnering Investor

God Pocket Investor

Great Commission Partner

Ministry Investor

Systematic Supporter

Financial Friend

Ministry Stock Holder

Joyful Intentional Investor

Purpose Partner

Your authors lean toward the *shareholder* narrative when speaking at fundraising events. However, shareholder, partner, and joyful intentional investor are great words that encompass God-instructed responsibility and cultural understanding. We will use [partnership] often for our go-to word in this writing, although the congregational companion book teaches tithing based on the Joyful Intentional Investment narrative. Find a tithe word or phrase that works for your audience? Though tithe has worked since circa-1600, language and culture are changing more rapidly than before. The internet has brought generations of cultural change in minutes. Partner or shareholder may be excellent words today but out-of- vogue by the end of this decade. Accept that. It is like the music services, we don't own the music anymore. We simply rent it for a season.

Language of Success

People want to join a winning team. In our non-profit fundraising world, we see organizations shoot themselves in their foot rather often. They produce an excellent narrative for need but do so in a way that makes the potential donor feel as if the only thing that separates the organization from bankruptcy is that potential donor's gift. Some churches talk so much about money, one would think they are going under on Sunday afternoon without it. Nobody wants to climb on board a sinking ship. People want to support success.

Perception is reality. If I perceive desperation, whether real or not, I will see you as a lost cause. I will not invest in loss.

How we articulate the concept of tithing or partnership must be done in a manner that doesn't seem as if we are grasping for our next breath. If you are grabbing for this breath, you will most likely be grasping and grabbing again for the next one. One might as well get the drowning over with. Success is a language that is received well by every generation. Speak about victories in finance in ministry, not defeat. Threats of closure only tell a donor that their past money was given in vain; thus their future gifts are of the same frivolous nature.

Basic Facts

We owe it to our listener to speak their language. There is nothing intrinsically spiritual about specific languages, such as Hebrew, Greek, Latin, Spanish, or English. Let's not treat our generation's English as if it is the official language spoken by the Father in heaven. *I do secretly hope it is.*

It is the teacher's responsibility to teach, not the listener's responsibility to learn. The teacher must create a lesson that allures interest and present our content in a way that captivates the audience's attention. We take issue with any belief that the listener-learner has all the obligation. We also believe that teachers should deliver honest insightful content and not just a happy homily.

We owe it to the current and future financial stability of our church to teach tithing. Teaching the ongoing necessity to support the church in repeated partnership financially is a good thing. Educating the whole truth of God's Law of Intentional Investment is honorable. Giving opportunity for our congregation to sow and reap is necessary. If we fail to teach this Jesus principle, we have missed a great truth of Holy Scripture and denied our very calling. Tithing by any chosen name is not just a good thing; it is a God thing.

Opposable thumbs allow us to grab tightly, but our thumb's muscular system was not designed for the thumb to hold indefinitely. A thumb is but a transfer device. A giver needs to give, and we are all givers. We do not see in scripture any special grace dispensation to certain people to be less-than-faithful partners in ministry. It is built into the core DNA of man to feel good when they give. We always feel good doing what we were designed to do. God is the ultimate giver: giving creation, giving life, giving us souls, giving us reconciliation through Christ, giving us eternity. We then, being made in the image of God, should emulate God-likeness on that point too.

Houston We Have a Problem

How can we learn to speak the ever-morphing language of this ever-changing culture? That is a great question. Beyond simple word replacement, if you are going to connect to parishioners, donors, and church clients in their heart-giving language, you must learn the secondary narrative language beyond the primary language. You must learn to deliver a narrative that connects with their wallet and their heart below, above, around, and inside the verbiage. You must learn to give secondary narratives as they are the subliminal understanding.

Every story has a primary narrative (N1), a basic story. Jesus used it. In every parable, He shared and we [all] heard the primary and basic story. But for some, our heart, mind, emotions listened to a deeper second narrative (N2). These stories inside the stories brought a deeper understanding to those who had ears to hear. Sometimes, even the ones who walked with Him daily had to say, "Umm, what did you mean by that?" They well knew that Jesus spoke in in-depth narratives (N2), beyond the outward story.

Every Jesus parable had a secret or hidden message bottled up inside a captivating story. That is what we pastors attempt to reveal every week to those who often have hearing/understanding trouble.

The somewhat dated children's book *The Velveteen Rabbit* is an excellent example of deeper narrative. Allow us to paraphrase these delightful talking stuffed animals. When the skin horse privately ask the rabbit what makes it so real and so loved by its child owner, you can get a glimpse into the secret narrative. The rabbit's response can bring tears to your eyes as it declares that real is something you become after your skin is rubbed off and loved off. You become real after an eye has been pulled off and sewn on. Reality is seen after you have been loved for a long time and your fur is matted. But once you are real to a child, you can never be ugly. Pardon our paraphrase. *Go buy the book and read it to your children and grandchildren.* Buried in the story is a message of truth that inspires powerfully.

We need to share illustrations and stories that show the result of people systematic giving through the local church.

I can share a story about a family that was helped by the church and wanted to thank those who were shareholders last Sunday. I can share a story about a car that was repaired and a job that was kept thanks to the generous systematic church financial partners. I can tell about the fifty people who received Christ through the church mission program and how those conversions points (hypothetically speaking) go to the heavenly account of the ones who made it happen, the faithful partners. The deeper narrative makes sure the audience feels thanked for their gift and successful in there gift. The deeper description helps them know their significance. And they are significant. What is your offering time messaging? What do the support illustrations given within your sermons articulate?

If Jesus put messages within His messages, should we not look at the most exceptional communicator of all time, at least the most quoted, and take something from His narrative and sub-narrative style? Would it be wrong for us to copy Him? Your parishioners might like it, as His sermons were rather short and very memorable. Think of the uproar if your sermon only lasted ten minutes and could be remembered years later. The congregation might revolt! Or they might give you a massive pay raise.

Narratives are more than changing a word from tithing to partnership or shareholding. Deeper narratives instill inspiration the hearts and souls of an audience to become cheerful partners in the ministry, not just obligated partners of the organization. And there is a big difference. We must use all of our pulpit conversations to motivate and disciple. Don't waste verbiage on fodder. Work hard to produce talks that encourage the listener to be a part of the winning team. Articulate how partners share in the God-given rewards!

Changing Your Reoccurring Narrative

How do we speak to our congregation and motivate them to tithe systematically? How do we teach partnership in this multi-aged culture?

"Being a Christian is more than just an instantaneous conversion. It is a daily process whereby you grow to be more and more like Christ." -Dr. Billy Graham[13]

We want our sons to take out the garbage on their own, and we continue to motivate them to do it until they develop the weekly garbage disposal discipline. When dealing with church members, you cannot threaten to take away their internet time! *Unless your church provides free internet.* Leaders have to motivate, encourage, disciple, and inspire them to do the right thing until it becomes their instinct. We all know the basic premise of discipleship. We will not belabor it here. The cumulative and residual effect of intentional tithing/shareholding stories and sermons will produce genuine systematic partners when we combine this with trust, transparency, and community.

Chose to implement this into your service times. We must move from thought to real action, intentional action, and planned action in our reoccurring narratives to have the cumulative and residual effect work. How long it will take to see results depends upon the quality of our narratives and the audience. Conversely, is there ever a time when you would want to stop your partnership narratives?

---

[13] https://billygraham.org/devotion/a-daily-process/

Look at Some Fundraising Professionals

How do the major charities, who do not possess the added motivation of biblical mandate (tithe), create urgency in giving? They do this by creating a message that moves people to be a part of a solution.

Much of our current tithe narrative is given as "because the Lord says to tithe." That answer will not work anymore. The Bible might also suggest that the woman should be under the control of the man. *Go home and tell your wife that and let's see how that goes.* The Bible might suggest that we take our disrespectful teenagers out and stone them. *Try that too, after you put your wife in place. You might want to keep some bears around to eat any neighborhood children who make fun of your hairdo or lack of hair.* That discipline is not continuing as well as some prophets might have hoped either. Just because something is in the Bible does not mean that it will be automatically followed. We know that in our own life as well.

The successful fundraiser tells a story, and tells that story quickly. Great fundraisers are expert 30- to 90-second narrators. Have you watched a St. Jude Children's Hospital commercial? Our families support them every year because they give us believable narratives of hope that our gifts will provide substantial success, and they do it in thirty seconds. They tell stories that inspire us and make us feel good about giving. And again, they do it in thirty seconds. In fundraising circles, it is commonly known that any video explaining your project that is more than three minutes long is most likely counterproductive. *As pastor guys, we refuse to check that time/productivity theory in connection to a sermon time length.*

If you want to teach like Jesus, you are going to have to learn how to tell stories, tell them quickly, and hide within them connections to the heart. You may have to trust the Spirit to reveal some of the truth without your voice attached. While walking on the roads, people would ask Jesus what seemed to be a simple question, and His answer began with a story. "A certain man had two sons..."[14] Within that very parable was the story of the prodigal's rebellion, the story of the Father's love, the story of the rotten heart of the seemingly good son, the story of the restoration provided by the servants of the father, the story of insanity going to sanity, and maybe even the story of the Storyteller who chose to relate to every class of people within His earshot. That is six stories in one. That is six weeks' worth of sermons if you're looking for good material. Most of us speak so long the average attendee can't remember what we said. Less is more in the advertising world. Less seemed to be more in every Jesus parable.

From Wikipedia: Narrative is found in all forms of human life. Oral storytelling is the earliest method for sharing narratives. During most people's childhoods, narratives are used to guide them on proper behavior, cultural history, the formation of a communal identity, and values. Narratives may also be nested within other narratives.[15]

---

14 C.f. Matthew 21:28.

15 https://en.wikipedia.org/wiki/Narrative

Paul Harvey became king of storytelling back when radio ruled the airwaves and televisions only had three channels. As the leading pitchman for ACE Hardware, Harvey's secondary narratives found themselves great human-interest stories, and his most infamous closing story would make you stop your car and roll up the windows with a manual hand crank to not miss a single word of it. He would take you up to the very pinnacle of the story and then stop to share an ACE Hardware commercial. He would finish the moving, inspirational story and deliver those words that some can still hear today, "And now you know the rest of the story." Paul Harvey understood and utilized secondary narratives.

Get your secondary narrative on! Perfect your honest, morally genuine, ethical, often subconscious encouragement that lingers just under the surface of any story or illustration motivating the listener to partner in the moral of the story. You will not find (N2) on the Oxford Word of the Year list. It's our word.

We All Want to Be Heroes

Often our giving scenarios create "Us and Them" mentalities. A pastor can tell of all the things he accomplished for the kingdom during the prior week, or he can tell of all the things that the church ministry partners were able to achieve in the last week through their tithing partnership. Pardon the use of tithing there. We are still breaking it loose slowly. It will disappear. Listen to the well-funded para-church world, and you will hear the word ministry partner used in every episode.

Christian Comedian Mark Lowry talked often about his boyhood experience when his father told bedtime stories. He and his brother were always the heroes of the story. How Mark, this little ADD brat, loved bedtime. He found himself the superhero in every story before he drifted off to dreamland. Does your offering time inspire people to be the, or does your offering inspire them to support you so that you can do great heroic things for God? Are the heroes of your church you or your financial partners?

> **"Humility is not thinking less of yourself, it's thinking of yourself less."**
> **-Rick Warren, Pastor**[16]

Secondary narratives (N2) draw a listener into the story. N2 makes the listener the hero of every story. If you cannot give up the lead role of Pastor Hero of your church, your congregation may soon let the hero be responsible for funding his hero- ness by himself. We are in an age where people want in on the deal. Our computers allow us to green screen ourselves into any scenario we desire. You can have your own personal designer jeans and shirts. Times are changing. If you think you can get people to watch you do great, heroic, Superman things and have those people continuously respond by giving you great money to do that, you will shortly learn a sad lesson about kryptonite. *And it bites hard!*

---

[16] https://www.goodreads.com/quotes/383930-humility-is-not-thinking-less-of-yourself-it-is-thinking

"It was pride that changed angels into devils; it is humility that makes men as angels."
-Saint Augustine[17]

We must show, through our exemplary oratory skills that we attained in our homiletics classes, the fulfilling joy it is to give and share and partner. Both of your authors have helped hundreds of Christian organizations improve their bottom line though inspiring greatness in partnership. We take the stage and inspire people, young and old, to join the productive, successful team. Inspiring is very different than convincing. It has an even lower threshold. However, inspired people positively get behind a project and stay behind it. When you follow through on that inspiration with phenomenal results, they become convinced. When that happens, you have partners for life.

We must speak inspiration to the soul, not threats from the law. In 2 Corinthians 3:6, Paul reminds us that the letter of the law kills, but the spirit of the law gives life. We must talk about the joys of giving and the life now rewards of partnership—and the eternal rewards of collaboration.

"Do you wish to rise? Begin by descending.
You plan a tower that will pierce the clouds?
Lay first the foundation of humility."
-Saint Augustine[18]

---

17 https://www.brainyquote.com/quotes/saint_augustine_148546
18 https://www.brainyquote.com/quotes/saint_augustine_148548

Consider this question: Was Jesus the reoccurring superstar of His own parables? This greatest of teachers was not the star of his own stories. He shared stories the listener could find themselves in: as the abused, the abuser, the broken, the captive, and even the hero. Jesus is the ultimate hero of the entire New Testament. He is the hero of eternity, but He remained the humblest of all leaders. Even Jesus gave all the glory to the Father.

In your relationships with one another, have the same desire as Christ Jesus: Who, being in very nature God, did not consider equality with God something to be used to his advantage; rather, he made himself a servant class, clothed in human likeness. In that appearance as a man, he humbled himself by becoming obedient to death on a cross. -Philippians 2:5-8 para

I remember watching an interview with a former SNL comedic performer. This jokester noted that his anti- religion views were never aimed at Jesus. Rather, as he perceived, the prideful, arrogant people who claimed to be like him. This comedic noteworthy rambled of Jesus never saying, "All those miracles ... Me! The blind eyes opened ... Me also ... Walked on the water ... Did you see Me? I was amazing! Water into wine? Yep, I did that." They went on to compare Christ's humble narratives to what he perceived to be the braggadocio attitude of the political religious machine. As a trained observer of life, comedians get it. People are tired of braggarts and mercenaries. They are tired of the paid heroes. True humility rocks! When we present a need, it must be accompanied with genuine gratefulness to the donor-partner-giver who is the hero of the gift. We must also give God the glory for the results the hero has had. There is little room left for ministerial middlemen seeking to bolster their self-serving credibility through the kindness of others.

What good is humility if people don't know you have it?[19]

It is interesting to us that John wrote in 1 John, chapter 3, "Behold, what manner of love the Father hath bestowed upon us, that we should be called the sons of God: therefore, the world knew us not, because it knew him not. Beloved, now are we the sons of God, and it doth not yet appear what we shall be: but we know that, when he shall appear, we shall be like him; for we shall see him as he is." Maybe John could have separated himself as the special one. But John, with all of his true greatness, brought the listener (us/we) into the story, into the prominence, into the inclusive partnership.

Thank You

Great fundraisers know how to start their message by thanking the people. If you don't correctly express genuine thankfulness, you will most likely not receive the gift again. People want to be thanked. People want to be thanked again. People love to be thanked multiple times. We all want to be acknowledged, even

---

[19] www.MikeWilliamsComedy.com

for small gifts. And small gifts do matter. In the years we have produced fundraisers for major faith-based organizations, we have yet to have a donor-partner stop partnering because we thanked them too often. God himself seems to be partial to those who are thankful.

"Thank you' is the best prayer that anyone could say. I say that one a lot. Thank you expresses extreme gratitude, humility, understanding."
- Alice Walker, Author[20]

How many times do we need to thank a donor? That question raises its ugly head at every workshop and training. The answer is always the same. It is somewhere between often and regularly and more-often.

Paul's letters to the churches
are all filled with repeated gratitude
and thankfulness for their support.
Paul knew how to articulate a proper thank you.
In doing so he received continued support.

We thank people upon their first gift. In a church situation, this can be after every offering time. It can be as he prepares to preach. Pastors need to thank the people for their kindness and generosity every week. Do you thank your people for making church possible? Start this Sunday. Repeat it every Sunday. Let

---

them feel a significant part and responsibility for what they are seeing around them.

Should we thank them for doing what they ought to do? Good question. Should people thank us for providing a great sermon when we certainly get paid to provide it? 2 Corinthians 9:7 might help us realize that we can thank people for their heart decision to give. Kindergarten class should have taught us that it's always right to say thank you.

"God has given us two hands—one to receive with and the other to give with. We are not cisterns made for hoarding; we are channels made for sharing." -Billy Graham[21]

A New Word for Your Mental Library

Fundraisers professionals often talk about wallet to plate (WTP) conversion. This is a possible projected amount assigned to an audience based on the expertise of the speaker and history of the donors. We could tell you with great certainty what would be the potential gift dollar amount for most any audience. This article is not about formulas and secular equations, although they do work for both secular and sacred situations. This knowledge is about the genuine, moral, and ethical discipleship of any congregation or group to give repeatedly to the church or a church-related project.

---

[21] www.brainyquote.com/quotes/billy_graham_589700

Laughter Giving

Does your church service approach the giving times in a positive, uplifting way? Really? Does the choir sing jubilantly in celebration, or is it always the somber instrumental tones of the piano reminding the younger ones that this is a time for seniors? Does your offering time make them question if this church the place to support as their future church?

Let each one give [thoughtfully and with purpose] just as he has decided in his heart, not grudgingly or under compulsion, for God loves a cheerful giver [and delights in the one whose heart is in his gift].- 2 Corinthians 9:7 Amplified Bible

God desires each of you should give what your heart can give in a joy-filled manner.
Feel free to invest and not compelled to pay.
-2 Corinthians 9:7 para

The late D. James Kennedy is rather famously known for his teaching on this verse. He claims the word cheerful in 2 Corinthians 9:7 is literally the word from which we derive the word *hilarious*, and thus we need to adjust the attitude in which we give our gifts and the tone in which we receive the gifts. If Dr. Kennedy is right, is your church meeting this hilarious offering design?

For God loves a hilarious giver.
- 2 Corinthians 9:7 para

A local Baptist pastor has taught his worship team to clap their hands every time the Deacon Of The Week prepared to deliver the offertory prayer. Initially, they found it cumbersome to transition into a clapping mode, considering most of the deacons carried with them the vocal excitement of sea slug. Nevertheless, as the deacon approached the microphone, the worship leader would announce, "We celebrate this opportunity to give back to the Lord a generous gift of gratitude for all He has accomplished in and through us." The worship team would start applauding. The congregation, not wanting to be left out, would follow. It caught on in this white middle-class church. Clapping is contagious. After ten years, everyone continued to clap for the offering time.

> *"It's enough to indulge and to be selfish, but true happiness is really when you start giving back."*
> *- Adrian Grenier, Actor*[22]

Is it wrong to create excitement about giving? Is it wrong to inspire the giver? Is it wrong to make giving joyful?

Inspire to Greatness

More than simple word changes of tithing to partner/shareholder and cultural nuances of plates to boxes, leaders need to [inspire] people to greatness in their giving. We must inspire them to believe they can do something of legacy value. We must inspire them to

---

22 www.brainyquote.com/quotes/adrian_grenier_432076

join together, give together, and pray together because they are the church. Together, the sum is greater than the individual parts.

Your authors serve together on a developing world mission project. We talk a lot about hope, helping, recue, and teamwork. Behind it all we know that we are more powerful together. Do your people feel that? We have all watched the clear and articulate way in which many para- church leaders envelop their partners into the success of the work. They are good at it. But let's get back to the real world of small and medium rural and suburban church life. Our call for financial partnership must be filled with honesty in saying, "This ministry happens because of you in the pew, not just me at the pulpit." At the very least, every pastor must emphasize the "we factor" in the giving. Anything shy of that will slowly erode the financial relationship. People want to know they matter and their gifts matter for something significant.

"No leader, however strong, can succeed at anything of national importance or significance unless he has the support and cooperation of the people he is tasked to lead and sworn to serve."
- Rodrigo Duterte, Filipino Statesman[23]

Very few of us would or could afford to remain at our church and do what we do if it were not for that check every week. We might have the desire to work for free, but our wives may be sending out resumes for us after the second week. Say what we will, we are all,

---

23 www.brainyquote.com/quotes/rodrigo_duterte_769524

by default, paid to play. Pastors, of whom we count ourselves, are like football stars. We get to do what we love and get paid for it. We need to shut up, get in the game, and score like the professionals we are. We need to lead our team to a winning season, and we need to do it humbly. We need our real life to reflect our on podium persona. In this illustration, it is good to take a knee occasionally.

QUESTIONS TO PONDER:

1. How has modern "Grace Theology" affected your people?
2. What new verbiage should you include for speaking to the current culture?
3. How is the "Thank You" narrative being used in your offering times?
4. How is your median congregational age demographic affected by modern culture?
5. Who is the "Hero" in your offering times?
6. Is your offering genuinely a time of joy and celebration?
7. How could your offering times become more celebration?

CHAPTER Seven
ARTICLE - Speaking Fluent Partnership

Businessman, Naveen Jain has said; "True philanthropy requires a disruptive mindset, innovative thinking, and a philosophy driven by entrepreneurial insights and creative opportunities."[24]

Your authors have raised millions of dollars using a straightforward presentation outline. This outline is more easily remembered using the simple acronym of STARPA. People of all ages understand and respond more generously when we:

- **Show** the need clearly, in as few words as possible.
- **Tell** an exact amount it will take to become a success.
- **Ask** for an immediate gift, prepared to receive funding in multiple ways.
- **Respond** immediately with proper thank you narrations.
- **Provide** evidence the project was successful.
- **Ask** again for the next project.

That outline does not need a lot of explaining, except for maybe the P. The questions always have to do with the latter point of providing evidence rapidly. How do organizations do that? Secular and larger para-church organizations do it because they are not living

---

[24] https://www.brainyquote.com/quotes/naveen_jain_517090

hand to mouth. Today's financial request is actually funding a future project, not the one they're asking for today. They realize that donors repeatedly give when rapid completion evidence is provided. People desire to know that their gift mattered. When their gift matters, they matter. It's all about significance, and significance is hugely impatient.

> *"Success is fine, but success is fleeting.*
> *Significance is lasting."*
> *-Beth Brooke, Businesswoman[25]*

Look at this STARPA example as used in a special project offering for an upgraded children church area.

- **Show the need**: "Most people make decisions for Christ before they turn 18. We need to expand our children's department to reach more children with the gospel of Christ. We want to make sure that when your kids, your neighbor's kids, or even your great grandkids walk into the children's department, they are blown away by Jesus." (Inspire the listener.)
- **Tell the exact amount: "**We need $400,237.00 to complete what we know will be the finest and most effective children's teaching place in our town. This place will excite children about following Jesus!"
- **Ask for an immediate gift:** "I need our church family to join together to save the children, and in doing so we save the future of

---

25 www.brainyquote.com/quotes/beth_brooke_615505

this church. I need you to make a significant investment. Not just significant in amount, but significant because of what these gifts will accomplish. In your hand, today is a response card. Some of you may be able to write a large check, while others will partner monthly for this God work. Together, we will take back what the enemy is trying to steal from us—our most precious treasure, our children. I have to admit special fundraisers scare pastors. I know that sometimes when new projects come, people forget the normal ongoing costs to operate the wonderful ministries that are already happening. So we will give today prayerfully. We are going to stop right now and talk to God. I want you to personally ask God to lead you in what He would have you give as your *Rescue the Next Generation Legacy Gift.* Will you be a hero for a child today?" (Of course, this church is prepared to receive those gifts via check, and credit card in our post-modern society. They are also prepared to receive automated reoccurring gifts with the simplest of paperwork for the donor.)

- **Respond immediately with a thank you:** The next morning, your support staff should be prepared to send out gratitude notes to everyone who gave. Thank them within three days, and you might receive an additional gift next week and the week after. Large donations need to be met with personal calls from the deacons, elders, or even the pastor himself.

- **Provide evidence rapidly:** You asked for money, so you'd better get busy building. The congregation needs to see some scaffolding in the north hallway and some drywall stacked by the door. Don't apologize for it. Use it as a reminder their gift is fulfilling the need and will soon touch lives.
- **Ask again for the next project:** No explanation is needed here.

Let us note that we did not title the project "Remodel A Children's Area." Remodel is not as powerful a word choice. Remodel says to fix the old. Rescue is more powerful and drips of success. We included the legacy word. People want to leave a significant legacy. We used a title that expressed the results of the project: Rescue the Next Generation Legacy Gift.

How could we use STARPA in a normal Sunday offering situation?

- **Show the need:** "The mission of First Church is to lead people to Christ and disciple the members to become more like Christ. Last year, we baptized thirty-four people in that pool behind me, and those people are here today and becoming powerful disciples. We have ministries with two foreign language groups in our community. We partner with twenty-one different missions around the world, bringing the gospel to the ends of the earth. Children are brought to Jesus, and students are given the ability to follow Jesus with their lives. I don't have the time to tell you what the heroes of First Church have done over the past thirty years. I do know that our legacy is still in the beginning stages. There are more who need Jesus. Every Sunday morning, we gather together, and the heroes of the church make it happen again through their financial partnership." (Inspire the listener.)

- **Tell an exact amount: "**Our budget is fairly low compared to other churches our size. I commend our budget committee for being wonderful stewards." (If your budget needs are significantly low share them. You could also share a cost per person. Build trust while you assure them the cost is well overseen.)

- **Ask for an immediate gift:** "As we bow to pray, I want to invite you to be a part of the victories that are seen through the members of First Church. I want to invite you to be a full shareholding partner in every ministry that goes out from these walls to save souls for Christ Jesus. Your partnership is making a significant difference, and according to Hebrews, chapter six, verse ten, "God will not forget the work you did or the love you showed for him in the help you gave and are still giving." When the plates are passed, will you join the amazing partners already changing our city and the world through First Church?"

- **Respond immediately with thank you:** The next morning, your electronic postings can declare the needed Sunday goal was met thanks to the phenomenal partners of First Church. The newsletter can claim victory. Make sure the heroes of the funding success are the ongoing partners, with an extra special nod to the first-time givers.

- **Provide evidence rapidly:** Share with your congregation a testimony of how First Church touched the life of someone in the neighborhood or around the world the very next week. Give them a reason to support you every week. Show yourself working with the money you are given.

- **Ask again:** Prepare your tithing-partnership narrative each week with greater understanding in mind. Never miss an opportunity to inspire your audience to invest significantly in your mission. Help them see their involvement in the Great Commission through their partnership.

Let's go back to line number one... Show The Need. Most of the time, we elongate the explanation of the need to the extent that our potential donors have no idea what we are really supporting. We often create 40-minute narratives that should be 40-second narratives. We create a ten-minute video that should always be under three minutes. Often we become ambiguous when it comes to placing a dollar amount on cost. We stammer and stall as if we are apologizing for telling God's people there is a need. We lose the listener's interest while trying to get ourselves comfortable asking for money. Your authors can tell you right now that we are paid grandly by organizations simply to ask clearly and quickly for partnerships. It is hard to do, and it is even harder to do very well. It is an art to do it spectacularly well while leaving the donor-partner feeling glad they have given and ready to give more at a moment's notice. This is why great fundraisers are paid very well. But the best news is that you can be one of those great fundraisers.

Never Ask for a Gymnasium

As good stewards before God, we would rarely fund your request for a gymnasium. We would support your desire to build a *Community Athletic & Discipleship Center* to meet the needs of your community or to fulfill the mission of the church. Look at the two sample narratives below:

NARRATIVE ONE:

"We have wanted to build a gymnasium for years. It was in the original drawings since our founding in 1974. We just never had the money, and we don't know, but since we aren't asking for anything else right now, it seems like the best time to do it. So, please support the building of a gymnasium. We are sure that a lot of families from the church would drive in from the suburbs and use it, and maybe even some businessmen would come over at lunch and use the walking track. We are not sure what the cost to operate the air conditioning or to pay a staff person would be. But all that will come in time. We need you to give toward the building first. If you build it, they will come. Amen?"

NARRATIVE TWO:

"Make a one-mile circle around this church, and you will find that less than four percent have a relationship to Jesus Christ—or even to this church. We want to change that. We want to fulfill the Great Commission responsibility. After much prayer and fasting, the elders have decided that an Athletic & Discipleship Center would be a wonderful way to reach families in our area and businessmen in our community. Understanding that over eighty percent of those who come to Christ do so during their teen years and knowing that over 1,250 teenagers are living within a mile of this proposed Athletic and Discipleship Center, we intend to use the building as an outreach to them through team sports. It will cost $750,000 to build this ministry center and operate it for two years. We will not build it until we have the funding to staff it properly. We believe that the cost to reach the local community and serve the students of the church is $100 for each person reached over the next twenty years. I need you to pray and ask God how many people you want to reach for Him in the next twenty years. I am hoping that everyone here can commit to reaching at least ten people. My wife and I are going to personally take on twenty people in a one-hundred-dollar monthly faith promise to this significant Great Commission project."

Choose Your Narrative

Both narratives presented what the board wanted to do. However, only one created a significant cause with an accessible solution. You will see people to give to either, but you're going to get more people to give to significant success than you are to simply build something big and expensive.

Will the seniors give to a gym that they will never play in? Will everyone feel that a "play" area is the best way to serve God? You must articulate a genuine narrative that meets needs with purpose and significance.

"No one has ever become poor by giving."
-Anne Frank[26]

Anything you are asking for should be continually connected to a significant result. Until your audience sees the vision clearly in their mind, they will not fully invest the invisible image seen only in your mind.

Timing is everything

Keep it short! Short! Short! Can you tell us a time when Jesus got long winded? What was His longest recorded sermon to a crowd? Think about the words *Sermon on the mount* for a clue. Set your stopwatch to go. Begin reading it slowly. How long did that take? Most of us can't introduce our topic in the time that Jesus

---

[26] www.goodreads.com/quotes/81804-no-one-has-ever-become-poor-by-giving

took to deliver his longest sermon. *Of course, the people back then were much better listeners, had a better sound system, and the graphics were of a much higher quality because they were outdoors. Yes, that was sarcasm.* Jesus used simple narratives (stories) in which the audience could identify within one of the characters.

Jesus used stories to speak to the people. Stories command interest. Only with the closest confidants was their greater detail.

In our para-church (PRC) fundraising book *How to Fearlessly and Successfully Ask for Money*, there is an amazingly simple outline provided to prepare you to present any message in seconds. The book dares to declare that any story can be fully articulated in just about any time length allotted. In fact, the shorter the better in our short attention span culture.

Five Statement Noah Story

Once upon a time, there was a very godly man named Noah, who taught his children the truth of Jehovah God, and lived an exemplary moral life.

Every day, he and his children witnessed the evil around them flourishing, but they remained faithful to the God they served.

One day, God spoke to Noah with instructions to build a boat to save himself and the animals of the world from a rapidly impending evil-purging divine flood.

Because of that, Noah built a boat, and loaded it with animals, as the evil people around him ridiculed his entire family and the God he served.

Until finally, God personally shut the door of the boat as forty days and forty nights of rain flooded the earth, destroying all but Noah's maritime family.

It does not get any simpler than that 5 statement outline. What are you going to say in the minimal seconds to hook a potential financial partner before they are distracted by the latest text coming across their phone on the internet you provide them. Some are distracted by the background motion video on your very own screen. Your A.D.D. friends will spend the entire sermon trying to figure out the video loop points. Use this simple sentence starter outline to rapidly explain any ministry or fundraising request.

Once upon a time... (a need point)

Every day... (greater detail)

One day... (point of action)

Because of that... (results of action)

Until finally... (ongoing success)

Read the following example of how to use this rapid story standardization for church presentations.

Five Statement Church Narrative

In the early seventies, Dover, Florida was an area without God, filled with alcohol, drug abuse, and generation of children bearing the burden of those bad choices.

One spring day in 1972, a small group of Christians partnered together to become a genuine mission to this community, and First Church was born.

Because of that commitment, over 1,000 people have come to Christ, hundreds of families have been transformed, and our entire area is different.

Every week, students are receiving life coaching and Christian discipleship, migrant labor families are being reached, and ESL classes are preparing disenfranchised people for good jobs that can support their family.

Until finally, behind those early planters have come an elite circle of great commission partners who have taken up the mission to continue reaching our community. We want you to join us, and to share in God's success at First Church.

Can you identify the simple , Once upon a time…, Every day…, One day…, Because of that…, Until finally… narratives in each sentence or statement?

Every person in church leadership should be able to explain your church history and vision to anyone who asks in this simple form.

A Five Statement Tithing Partnership

Fourteen years ago, my wife and I began enjoying the First Church family, the inspiration, and the many excellent programs.

Every week, we would try to give a few dollars to feel that we were doing something.

One day we realized that being part of First Church is a partnership with God and with His people, and we began to give in a systematic way.

Because of that increase, we began to see what our partnership gifts were providing, and we noticed the portion we were giving was miraculously coming back to us.

Now, we are filled with joy every time we hear of a child or youth coming to Christ, as we realize that we had a part in that.

Notice how this narrative stayed very close to our standard five starter words. Notice how this narrative felt free to be creative when needed. Less is more! Less is more! Less is more! The truth is we needed to say that fewer times.

Wouldn't a story like this one make your listener want to be part of tithing? It was simplicity and peer pressure and promise rolled into a voice other than the voice of a pastor. Can we do this once a month before the offering time? Do our partnership narratives captivate people or castrate people? Every person in your leadership team should be able to share this similar style tithing narrative.

A Five Statement Testimony Narrative

At eighteen, I found myself living amid an alcoholic & drug abusive family. There was no safety, and I eventually found myself pregnant after being raped by a relative.

Every day the bus drove past your big First Church sign on the way to my work.

One Sunday morning, I came and sat in the back and listened. The people made me feel welcome, and when the invitation time came, I received Christ into my heart.

The beautiful people here welcomed me into a discipleship group and helped me get my life back on track.

Tonight, I stand here grateful for those who have made this church possible, as my life is has been transformed from heartbreak to hope. Thank God for His salvation, and thank you for bringing it to me.

This simple outline can be used to share needs, share offering stories, share tithe stories, and share blessing stories. An entire sermon can be taught using it. How could great testimonies presented in this short form encourage your partners to give every week? Here is the replacement for your deacon offering prayer! Think about this... If you could get everyone on your staff to present their ideas in this 5 line manner, you would cut your staff meeting time by hours. *This outline is a presentation outline for life. We think every church staff, deacon, and even church member ought to have their faith story available to be delivered in this manner.*

We use this outline for our foreign mission trips, preparing students and adults to share their faith story. It works.

Take a moment and write your tithe or faith story:

Once upon a time… (a need point)

Every day… (greater detail)

One day… (point of action)

Because of that… (results of action)

Until finally… (ongoing success)

Preachers Preach

We are very aware that our giftings as authors and preachers make us very prone to extrapolation. We have spent years in college and seminary. We have mastered the fine art of homiletics equipping us to take a text a small as John 11:35 and share it in a little less than an hour. We have letters after our names, which somehow require us to break into extended and footnoted articulation with the occurrence of any theological or non-theological question. For us to understand the power of a few sentences, it might be easier for a rich man to go through the eye of a needle. Nevertheless, when we can master the ability to inspire our short attention spanning culture with few words, those few words might change their life.

It is evident (from the brevity of his recorded sermons) that Jesus did not have any modern day homiletics training. He was much too brief.

Let us also be aware that many of these pre-offering narratives are going to be delivered by voices other than our own. So at very least we can master the principles to teach others how less can be more when cultivating a generous church.

Sharpen Your Sword

We are called to inspire. Whether you use a five-line offering narrative or a twenty- minute theological tithing dissertation, make sure that you inspire the audience to greatness. All the bullet points in the world do not match the motivation of hearing a passionate presentation and envisioning yourself as the hero of that presentation. Jesus told stories that his audience could relate to, see themselves in, or hope to be a part of. Jesus inspired the person with paralysis to be forgiven, to get up and carry his mat, and to go home.

Jesus inspired the tax man to come down from a tree and provide him with a good meal, then inspired him to believe that things could be different for him. Jesus inspired the prostitute to believe that she could be restored and looked at with compassion instead of judgment. *If we are to model Jesus, we need to be the most [inspiring people] on this ever-spinning terra firma.*

Both of your authors speak weekly for church and para-church organizations who are attempting to raise large sums of money. We both have an arsenal of inspiring stories. Let us share two that we have used in various fundraising situations. They are both well-known stories. We are betting you know at least one of them. Inspirational fundraising stories do not have to be well-kept secrets, as familiarity can be your friend. Familiar stories are most easily understood and often beloved by the listener.

Look at the following two stories recently used for an adoption fundraiser. The cause itself matters little; the closing can be altered to serve most any purpose.

Saving Starfish

A strange tide had left thousands of starfish stranded on the beach. The starfish were rapidly drying out and quickly dying out.

A man walking along the boardwalk noticed a another man, shoes off, pants rolled up, bent over in the sand picking up starfish one by one, and walking them out to the open water. Our boardwalk walker looked at the shoeless man, and he looked at the thousands of starfish. He thought to himself how small of an effect this starfish do-gooder was having. He was only one man, and there were far too many starfish for him to save.

Indignation rose within him, and he yelled out his observation to our starfish rescuer, 'Hey there, man! There are too many starfish out there. You can't save them all.' To which the hero of our starfish story looks up, but only briefly to respond, 'You're right, I can't save them all, but I can save this one.' And he placed yet another starfish into the saline waters of the sea and saved another life.

Tonight, I am going to ask you to save the life of one child and transform the life of one family. The cost to do that is a simple gift of one dollar and ninety-seven cents a day to accomplish this task over the course of one year. Two dollars moves each of us from being the critical passerby to becoming the hero—the hero of a real-life rescue story. Will you be the hero for a child today?

Moses and Susan

Many of you are old enough to remember the Paul Harvey radio program. He told wonderfully captivating human-interest stories. Those great stories that would drag your ear toward the radio. Then, when you were just about to find out the mystery name of the story, he would launch into an ACE Hardware commercial. They were the sponsors of his program. After that short reminder about the deals of the week at ACE, this master storyteller would reveal the name of the person behind the story. He closed each week with an iconic line. A line that has left a legacy in radio history as his voice became staccato, "And... now... you... know... the rest of the... story."

Maybe that is why I love the story of Norman Borlaug. You may be saying, 'Who is Norman Borlaug?' At Borlaug's 90th birthday celebration, Colin Powell said, "Countless millions who will never know his name will never go to bed hungry because of him."

Borlaug was born and raised in Cresco, Iowa, and educated in a one-room schoolhouse. In the 1940s, he pioneered the development of special wheat that was more efficient and had more excellent resistance to disease. He is credited today with saving the country of Mexico from famine. Norman Borlaug's lifelong innovations and developments are believed to have saved over two billion lives.

At the grand age of 90, he had not given much thought to retirement, saying, "I hope I can continue to be productive and die with my boots on."[27]

---

[27] abcnews.go.com/WNT/PersonOfWeek/story?id=131587&page=1

WOW. Two Billion lives saved. Talk about a world changer! What Colin Powell failed to mention was that without Henry Wallace, there would never have been a Norman Borlaug.

You may be wondering who is Henry Wallace? Let's do a little history refresher. Franklin Roosevelt served four terms as US president, and from 1941 to 1945, that was Henry Wallace. While Wallace was vice president, he used his authority to create a laboratory in Mexico, whose purpose was to create that hybrid wheat and corn that was needed to save the country. Though faced with heated debate for political based appointees, Wallace charged the young botanist, Norman Borlaug with the daunting responsibility of feeding the third world.

Norman Borlaug may have won the Presidential Medal of Freedom and the Nobel Prize and had Colin Powell at his birthday party, but Henry Wallace was the guy who fought to bring the right man to the project that saved billions.

But wait. Maybe it was not Henry Wallace. Perhaps it was George Washington Carver. Everyone remembers him. He is the man who gave us peanut butter. Where would the peanut butter and jelly sandwich be without him? It would just be the jelly sandwich, an unbalanced clump of purple sugar on bread. A diabetic dilemma! George Washington Carver went on to create 266 other peanut-driven products we still use today and so much more.

George Washington Carver needs to be mentioned because he went to Iowa State University. Carver would go on weekend botanical field trips to learn everything he could about his chosen field. His dairy sciences professor encouraged his son, Henry, to join Carver on those field trips. I'll bet by now you can guess which young life George Washington Carver was directing in those formative years. It was Henry Wallace.

So, the two billion lives need to be credited to George Washington Carver then, right? Wait just a minute. I've got to introduce you to Moses.

Moses and Susan lived in Diamond, Missouri during dangerous times for equality thinkers. This young couple believed that all men are created equal, and they demonstrated it by not having slaves, though living in a slave state. Their beliefs made them a target for the maniacal Quantrill's Raiders, who used their political view to justify their raping and burning and killing. One night, the Raiders rode through Moses' and Susan's area. These outlaws burned several buildings, shot innocent people, and drug off Mary, a young black woman carrying a young son named George.

Without delay Moses and Susan went about getting the word out to find Mary and her infant child. Mary had been murdered by the raiders, but for some they had reason kept the child alive. Through nothing shy of a miracle, a meeting was secured between Moses and the Raiders.

Moses rode his only horse for many hours to that dark southern Kansas crossroads. It was lit only by the torches of Quantrill's Raiders. Moses traded his transportation, his only horse, for a rough burlap sack containing a motionless body of a child. As the Raiders rode off into the night, Moses opened sack to find a shivering, nearly dead, naked baby boy. He wrapped the child under his clothing and started a twelve- hour [walk] home. The child lived.

They raised the child and gave the child a passion for learning. Sent that child of Mary's to school and then onto Iowa State University, where as a young student he took field trips with impressionable young minds.

Maybe it was Moses and Susan who should receive the Nobel Prize and the Presidential Medal of Honor. Perhaps it was Moses and Susan who saved two billion people on a cold Kansas crossroad a long time ago.

If we could go forward into time, how many lives could we touch tonight? Tonight, we are all offered the unparalleled opportunity to rescue a child too. Tonight, we are all offered the opportunity to be the hero of the life-saving story. Through a partnership of one dollar and ninety-seven cents a day for one year, we can know that one child will be rescued solely by us. One child will be our legacy of life.

We either inspire to greatness or bore to apathy.

These narratives could have been used to build a Community Athletic and Discipleship Center, fund a program, or build an orphanage in Costa Rica. Let's use our stories and narrations to make a financial difference in the funding for every good work. Let's inspire our people to greatness in life, family, and financial shareholding partnership. It is the Jesus way.

QUESTIONS TO PONDER:

1. How would you rate the inspiration quotient of your last Sunday's offering narrative?
2. What change will you make to next Sunday's offering narrative?
3. How could you create an original offering request that uses the STARPA outline next week?
4. How could you replace illustration or story from your last sermon, making the listener the hero of the illustration?
5. Can you think of any place where you could use the five line narrative in other church presentations?

CHAPTER Eight
ARTICLE: What? Where? When?

Anybody can point out a problem. Most are better at pointing problems out than they are at fixing them. Bringing to light our financial issues is not our sole intent. We intend to equip you to grow your financial resources and use them to build the kingdom of God. Let's look at some rubber-meets-the-road applications for everyday church stewardship life.

Repetition is the best teacher.
Say it, repeat it, and illustrate it in multiple ways.
Then inspire the student to teach it.

We chose a teacher's version of this quote, but it goes back to the earliest of known writing. *Repetition is the best teacher.* If a pastor, finance committee, or para-church leader thinks that there is a single-shot narrative fix for their financial woes, they are sadly mistaken.

"I believe giving back is one of the greatest life lessons we can teach our children: that the world isn't all about them and that, through our actions, people will really discover what kind of a person we truly are." - Gretchen Carlson, Television host[28]

If you are going to greatly improve your congregation's wallet to plate conversion, you are going to have to work at it the same way you work at

---

28 www.brainyquote.com/quotes/gretchen_carlson_838615

their discipleship in any other area—repetition. The discipleship of tithing and partnership is caught more than it's taught.

Let's ask an internal question. Do you model giving, tithing, and partnership? We can't teach what we don't live. Personally, do we give joyfully or because it is the expected thing to do, or required by our denomination? Do we teach it to our children away from the pulpit?

"Let us not be satisfied with just giving money. Money is not enough. Money can be got, but they need your hearts to love them. So, spread your love everywhere you go."
- Mother Teresa of Calcutta[29]

A good advertising company knows the benefits of repetitive product placement. Let's refer back to the Wayne's World[30] movie for consistency of humor. All through the film were blatant and laughable product placements for several companies—Fender Guitars and Tim Horton's Donuts, to name two. If Madison Avenue understands how to place subliminal messages into a 15-second commercial, a 22-minute sitcom, or a 90-minute movie, why can't we?

Consider how to place creative partnership funding narratives strategically into your sermons, your announcements, your music, and your testimonies.

---

29 www.goodreads.com/quotes/58066-let-us-not-be-satisfied-with-just-giving-money-money?page=2
30 https://www.imdb.com/title/tt0105793/trivia

Weekly Sermons

Include in your weekly sermon a story with narratives that demonstrates how someone in your church financially supported a cause, and there was a great result. Make your partners the heroes of your sermon illustrations. There is always an internal fight to prove our [personal] worth by telling what we did, but we must fight this demon. Our sermon illustrations need a Batman and a Robin. God is always Batman, and your audience needs to be the Robin character as often as possible.

Henry Blackaby's book *Experiencing God* [31] teaches us to join our God, who is already working. Lead the appeal to join God and tell the congregational God stories. Find ways to ask for their testimonies. Could you have a phone extension that allows the congregation to share their God stories? Use your pulpit (coffee table) time to reinforce the team aspect of your mission and the success of your church. Replace the I with You. Use your sermons to praise the financial partners while avoiding the opportunity to berate the monetary scrooges. We [can] talk about good without having to chide the slackers.

Business Meetings

Present all your money matters in a positive light. Nobody wants to give to a losing team or a business that is failing. People provide a genuinely winning

[31] https://blackaby.org/experiencing-god/

team whatever that team desires. Talk about the victories, not the defeats. Rid your reports of pie charts showing electric bills and lawn care expenses. Is the electricity needed for ministry? If it is, it is a ministry. To a church, everything they do is part of the ministry. If the front yard was grown over like a jungle, it would speak volumes about your church leadership and your faith. Yard care is part of the ministry.

For almost two decades we have consulted with pro-life organizations who were trying to raise money based on the narrative that they needed funding because 1.8 million children were being aborted every year. That statistic certainly is tragic. When we convinced these organizations to base their funding request narratives on the number of children they were saving as opposed to losing, and sharing the exact cost of rescuing one child from that group, their funding numbers radically improved. Some improved by as much as 300% in a single year. Burger King does not welcome you to their restaurant by telling you that McDonald's outsells them ten to one. Neither do they threaten bankruptcy if you fail to use the drive-thru window every afternoon.

We have watched with sadness as organizational fundraising narratives proclaimed their doors would be closing if people did not give immediately. These organizations quickly found that people were less concerned about their doors closing than they had thought. People will not invest serious money in sinking ships. People vibrantly support the ships that are winning the regattas.

People don't give because you have needs. They give because you meet needs and they want to be a significant part of that success.

Financial announcements need to present giving opportunities with victorious outcomes, not warnings of impending doom. Shower your partners with praise for being part of a winning team. Do this at every business meeting.

Social Media

Build social media viewers to create additional streams of discipleship for all your inspirational topics. These additional streams of discipleship will generate an opportunity for further financial partnership encouragement and lead to improved revenue. Pastors often complain they do not have enough time to disciple their people while letting a daily audience walk away due to lack of electronic connection. These electronic mediums can be your key to more teaching time with your people. If you can master the art of the five-line sermon, you can give them Jesus-style (and length) messages every day. His style worked then and has proven itself to have long- lasting effectiveness. Though we love the great masters (Spurgeon, Wesley, and Whitefield, Moody), we have yet to meet anyone who has their entire sermon on a wall plaque or commented to memory. Jesus parables should inspire us in brevity.

Use social media posts to uplift and congratulate the victors of every church ministry and thank them for their weekly support. Thank your listener/watcher for being a hero of the church.

Create a template for your social media audience. When you create a template system, you will find it much easier to create a proper daily post. You can create many of your posts a week or month before. Never try to produce them all in real time. Consider the following possible schedule:

- **Monday - Praise Day** - Post praise reports about Sunday success stories, salvations, and decisions of merit. Remind your audience of the great part they play in the victory of the Sunday service. Thank them for their partnership.
- **Tuesday - History and Photo Day** - Post photos of church events in the past years, past month, or previous week. People love to find themselves and their friends in photos. Include photos of the church in its early days. Remembrances allow people to rejoice in the growth they have made happen. Take a photo (selfie) with a different class or group every Sunday and post it on Tuesday.
- **Wednesday - Information Day** - Post reminders of service times and invitations to be a part of special events. Have some special events. Nothing looks bleaker than a church calendar with nothing on it. Who wants to give ten percent of a weekly income to a church whose total service time is only one hour of their one-hundred-and-sixty-eight-hour week? That is not an equitable percentage in

anybody's accounting. The new normal for special events is they can cost you nothing. Any reputable artist or speaker will use their influence to bring in the crowd. They will share their income (ticket or offering) with the church. It is time your special events paid for themselves.

- **Thursday - Brag Day** - Post a mid-week praise report. Brag on the Wednesday-night attendees and those who came to practice for Sunday worship. Post a photo from Wednesday night.

- **Friday - Fun Day** - Post the "Pastors Joke of The Week" or funny internet picture of the week. Show your non-pastoral side for a minute.

- **Saturday - Partnership/Ownership Prep Day** - Post a great story about successful financial church partnership leading to a great victory. Prime your audience to come excited to give on Sunday. Your narrative does not have to be a Bible verse or quote from a known religious figure.

- **Sunday Morning - Wake Up** - Make their text beep with a message calling them to church. The text is the new church bell. Ring it! People will sleep through a hurricane but will wake up to see who might be tweeting them at three in the morning. Send them a picture of you holding a sign saying, "I can't wait to see you this morning." Get creative.

Release your Facebook posts multiple times a day to get your message read by Facebook players. Ask your congregation to "follow" the church posts. Always be encouraging. Electronic messages move people in many directions, good or bad.

At the time of this writing the social media platform Facebook is significantly limiting the circulation of plain [text style] messages, preferring photos and videos for more massive distribution. This company is currently giving the most significant distribution to [live video] streams. Use [live stream] video for higher delivery rates. Learn what the current social media algorithms are doing to your postings and work the system.

Look at your electronic messaging. Does it contain a narrative of stewardship encouragement? Newsletters (paper or electronic) need to feature success stories of partnership. Note when your messages will arrive. Never set a newsletter to arrive on Monday or Friday. Those times are too busy, and your newsletter will go into the trash. Always design the church newsletter to arrive in the morning. Give it an entire day in the inbox to be read.

Social media can be the daily discipleship of the post-modern generation. Get a camera, get a tripod, get on board. A pastor or para-church leader who does not take full advantage of this connection giant will soon find that his listeners are listening and supporting a pastor who does.

Be aware of the keywords that limit your distribution. Various social media platforms frown on words that lead people to act. At the time of this publication, Facebook algorithms will automatically lower the number of people who read your post if the posting asks for the reader to SHARE, REPOST, VOTE, or COMMENT. They want responses to be organic and not contrived. Know how your words affect your distribution.

Giving Narratives of Interest

Some chose to use encouraging quotes to express and stimulate generosity. Although quotes should not be used for every partnership narrative, they can be a pleasant change of pace. Below are a few we have seen used in newsletters and social media.

"Where there is charity and wisdom, there is neither fear nor ignorance." -Francis of Assisi[32]

"You may have heard of Black Friday and Cyber Monday. There's another day you might want to know about: Giving Tuesday. The idea is pretty straightforward. On the Tuesday after Thanksgiving, shoppers take a break from their gift-buying and donate what they can to charity." -Bill Gates, Microsoft[33]

"The life of a man consists not in seeing visions and in dreaming dreams, but in active charity and in willing service." - Henry Wadsworth Longfellow[34]

---

32 www.brainyquote.com/quotes/francis_of_assisi_392040

33 www.brainyquote.com/quotes/bill_gates_626164

34 www.brainyquote.com/quotes/henry_wadsworth_longfello_389748

"Be ever watchful for the opportunity to shelter little children with the umbrella of your charity; be generous to their schools, their hospitals, and their places of worship. For, as they must bear the burdens of our mistakes, so are they in their innocence the repositories of our hopes for the upward progress of humanity."
-Conrad Hilton, Businessman[35]

Let's Review

Without exception, we will all create an offering time that is the most joyful part of the service. Our most exceptional music will be served. The choir will sing joyfully as we contemplate our generous God and write checks or complete our partnership in electronic form together as one body. Giving is worship, deserving the same focus, respect, and celebration that any other part of our worship deserves. Pass the plates some Sundays and bring the offerings to the front on other Sundays. Encourage the parents to bring the children with them to give. The children love to participate, and it builds in them the joy of weekly giving. Giving in a public manner encourages everyone to be a part. Peer pressure can be a great motivator and discipleship tool when used with good intentions.

"Tithing is a bad ceiling but an excellent floor."
- John Ortberg, Author[36]

---

35 www.brainyquote.com/quotes/conrad_hilton_680938
36 www.brainyquote.com/quotes/john_ortberg_679378

Could you place a ship's bell on top of your offering box? Have a time where everyone goes to those boxes in celebration. God loves a cheerful, hilarious giver. Ding-ding! That may be *too much* for some of us. We understand, but we do question why we choose to meet giving with such anti-celebrational sentiment.

We can successfully receive offerings from younger generations. An electronic offering portal is standard fare for churches who seek to reach anyone who is technologically savvy. That technologically savvy demographic can be eight to eighty. Remember, seeing an offering portal in the narthex might make a younger visitor see you as hip rather than hip-broke and needing a walker. And for those churches who are tech-savvy enough to be podcasting or live streaming, there's an entire audience out there who may wish to give. Having that ability to financially partner online goes a long way, in that case. Some will find additional revenue streams from online watchers living hundreds of miles away.

Introduce the offering as a dignitary entering a room. Always introduce the reasons for receiving the offering with a good narrative. One might say, "Look around you. Everything we have at our disposal is a gift from God through our partners seated next to you. All of the ministry that goes on all week long—the salvations, the visitations, the discipleship, the ministry—it all happens because of wonderful people who have chosen to partner with God through our weekly offerings. You people are amazing. Thank you. And now let us thank God for each of our ability to give back to Him."

Inspire people to be a part of a systematic partnership. Never confuse pre- offering narrations with teaching on tithing. Often, churches attempt to have a leader or deacon give a short pre-plate passing dissertation on the [Biblical mandate] to the congregation. A congregation is inspired by last-ditch efforts with as much excitement as a root canal. In this multi-aged, post-modern society, people want value for their dollar. One might think to use this offering time to let them know the successes of last Sunday's tithes, offerings, and partnerships so that they might trust you with another round of dollars.

Speaking of Offertory Prayers

Unfortunately, we often use our deacons and elders to do the offering prayer. We say "unfortunately," because this prayer often showcases the poor prayer skills (articulation abilities) of our deacons and elders. *You all know what we mean.* Move your required deacon prayer to another time, because you consider the offering time to be significant enough to put your best foot forward. Never put a bad foot forward at any time, unless that bad footed deacon is a very generous tithing multi-millionaire!

Now, about those pre-offering prayers. Before you get judgmental or indignant, may the pastor who has never spiked his prayer with a sermon point, scripture reading, or spontaneously remembered illustration cast the first stone. May the pastors who never transitioned from "Dear Lord" to "And don't forget my final point as it says in Matthew chapter five..." get additional stones ready for subsequent launch. We have all moved at times from talking to God to talking about God with the audience. We have yet to meet a pastor who did not include messages to the people along with their conversation with God. So be careful in your critique of our next thoughts.

Forgive the honesty

Let's look at two example prayers that a parishioner might hear delivered before the average church offering time:

Prayer example 1: "Lord, Heavenly Father, God, Lord, Jesus, Lord, we thank you for the tithes, the ten percent that was ordained by You from the time that Abraham paid a tenth to Melchizedek, and even thus now until this day. May it be used to honor You Lord, Heavenly Father, God, Lord, Jesus, and Your work here at First Church. Be with our missionaries serving in foreign fields. Bless those serving in children's church and bless all the other churches in our community. Bless the gift and the giver and especially bless all who can't give Lord, Heavenly Father, God, Lord. We give our tithes and offering to you now Lord. Help the church to use it wisely. And help us be able to meet the budget this week as we have been a little down lately. Amen."

Prayer example 2: "Heavenly Father, we celebrate those who came to Christ this week at First Church. Bless these shareholding partners in front of me now whose generous financial partnership makes happen every week. We thank you for using them to supply the needs of our fourteen missionaries every month. We thank You for using them to provide for those the poor in our neighborhood, and the needs of the widows in this very congregation. Father, I am humbled to be surrounded by people who support this church by their sacrifice and their service. Together we will stand on the promises of your Word, looking forward to our promised reward. Amen and amen."

Which example prayer expressed a genuine attitude of thankfulness to God in preparation for receiving tithes and offerings? We all know that even the narrative of our prayer interacts with the heart language and minds of those listening. If they are to pray with us and add their "amen" along with ours, let's make sure that we lead them to "amen" the right things!

> ### Our words have enormous power.
> ### Use each of them wisely.

If you have those detestably monotonous deacons, move them to the opening prayer, where you have an entire service to make up for it without having to issue a written formal apology in the weekly bulletin. *We say that humorously, and seriously, of course.*

> ### "These for a show make lengthy prayers,
> ### and one day they will be punished most severely."
> ### -Jesus, Mark 12:40 para

By no means are we suggesting prayers of pretense. We are asking for the opposite. We are elevating our offertory prayers to be legitimate requests that have [intelligent thought] put into them. We will not approach our great God without something to actually say. We consider His greatness and prepare to speak to Him as we would a dignitary of the highest degree. We will call Him by His name and not ramble every deity reference we can recall. We chose not to stutter and stammer as one who has not talked to this dignitary before.

One might think this honor and preparation should be the standard anytime we go before the king to speak for the congregation. Never confuse unplanned improvisational prayer with holiness.

Because We Ask Not

Look in a slightly different atmospheric direction. Would you be willing to pause silently before the offering, or even kneel? Could you ask your congregation to silently pray and specifically ask the Heavenly Father how He would have them participate in supporting the work of the church? Could you ask them to remain on their knees until they know that He has spoken to them about a specific gift amount? No tithe sermon. No promise of 100-fold blessing. No name it - claim it. It is gutsy. But when people are willing to ask God and listen, good things—in fact, God things— happen. Could you let the God of the still small voice speak to the heart? We have used these silent "ask God" moments all over the country to raise millions. God speaks... and God inspires. We wholeheartedly believe it can work for you. Give people time to think and contemplate their gift.

"Words have energy and power with the ability to help, to heal, to hinder, to hurt, to harm, to humiliate, and to humble."
-Yehuda Berg[37]

We have a pastor friend who frequently asks his audience to lift their wallets, purses, and checkbooks before God and ask Him how much of it He wants back. Gutsy, yes! Many would struggle to raise their purse above their head. Other would be afraid to raise their hands in church for fear of being called a Charismatic.

Who Is In The Detail?

A friend of ours is a former writer for Veggie Tales and currently works in the Hollywood mainstream. He is the salt and light in a dark place. Our friend is often hired by a very large Christian fundraising organization. Many reading this book do not have the income level to have been invited to their exclusive multi-millionaire-only fundraising events. They fly only the wealthiest church members to exclusive places, at which time they entertain, inspire, and dine them well. They bring in the best known Christian artists, authors, and political. After a thorough warming period, they present opportunities

---

37 www.brainyquote.com/quotes/yehuda_berg_536651

for these special people to partner with large-dollar ministry projects. They use a basic STARPA outline.

It is rather impressive the amount of preparation they require and detail they routinely critique. Our friend, who is often employed as their humorous emcee, was brought in and asked to change the way he prayed. Was he saying something wrong, unscriptural, or theologically unsound? No. He was [exhaling] as he spoke the word "God," and they felt it was not in keeping with their overall approach. Yes, his [exhaling] was critiqued. You may think this is over the top and supercritical. In defense, this organization will raise twenty million in a single weekend because they pay attention to every little detail of what their people are communicating to the well-chosen audience.

We are not advocating for breath control here. We are using this illustration as a unique reminder that success is in the details. If you as a leader do not take control of the stewardship narratives, they will slowly dwindle to monotonous. *There are lots of groups detailed and energized enough to take your people's money if you don't make the effort.* Take authority and responsibility for your offering times. Treat them with the respect they deserve. Treat them as finely as you do your best sermon for your best audience. *Like the week the DOM, the Bishop, or the General Overseer is visiting!*

Where Is the Sovereignty?

After sharing this last illustration, we are in a slight struggle. Do we dare orchestrate the minutest points of the prayer, or anything else, as if it is not entirely up to the sovereignty of God? We understand that struggle. All we can prove at this time is the sovereignty of God in large dollar donations seems to be undeniably connected to preparation and details. Details matter to people, and even more to wealthier donors. Maybe details even matter to God. The minuscule difference between talking to a rock and striking a rock sure did change the outcome for a great leader named Moses. Think about it.

A Next-Level Partnership Club

Some churches and organizations have created an exclusive club for higher- level donors. *Ouch, that sounds very televangelist.* Nevertheless, we are not knocking them, because their daily television cost rivals what many churches operate on in a full year. Maybe they know something about fundraising that many don't.

"I would never have been able to tithe the first million dollars I ever made if I had not tithed my first salary, which was $1.50 a week."
-John D. Rockefeller[38]

In our book *The Whatever Life Hack* (Renovate Publishing), a story is shared about a couple that increases their tithe by one percent every year. Are they crazy? We think not. This hard-working couple has been doing this increase for over twenty years. They still run their mom and pop business together. There is no branding budget, no fanfare, no television commercials, just repeated yearly increase. They live

---

38 www.christianpf.com/john-d-rockefeller-quote-on-tithing/

very humbly compared to how they could live, but they still have time for a lot of trips, and a second home in Florida Keys. He and his wife enjoy their life and their children. They follow the Biblical outline for intentional joy-filled investing in the local church!

Have you considered calling people to a higher level in giving? It might not need to be one percent a year, but it could be a calling to something more. We like the name *Eleven Percent Club*.

On A Personal Note

Nobody can teach what they don't model. In the church/para-church fundraising banquet world, we have several statistical axioms that we fully understand. For example, a banquet event table with eight women will average slightly under $700 in donations. A table with four married couples (also eight people) will average $2,500 or more in donations. On average, a table with four pastors and their wives will produce promises to have a mission committee consider their organization for a monthly gift at a future date, along with a few twenty-dollar cash gifts. We apologetically explain this is because the pastors are bombarded by requests for money, whereas the rest of us are not. Maybe that is true. Perhaps we are merely trying to protect the good name of our own kind.

Seeing this material is written primarily to pastors and church leaders, we can speak freely. We should be the model of giving we would want from our partners. We can't genuinely teach what we don't live. And for the record, everyone in the world is bombarded by requests for money these days, including non-pastors.

If you have an email or social media account, you are already on a Charity hit list!

Single-Statement Partnership Narratives

These types of narratives are inspirational for a newsletter, a blog, a Facebook post, video post, or even in preparing your audience for the offering time.

- Janie was five years old when she climbed on the church bus. Today, she is teaching the fifth-grade girl's class. You better believe that your financial partnership with God at First Church matters.
- Show me someone who gives faithfully in the offering plate, and I will show you a person of genuine faith. It seems that money is the place where true faith is proven. Indeed, a person is not a Christian because they give, but they give because they genuinely believe, and they demonstrate it with what the world holds to be of utmost importance.
- People don't even see old signs. Our new sign helps people realize that we are here. Thank you to everyone who partnered to provide our new sign. You are amazing.
- Today, we gave a pair of shoes to a mother so that her child could go to school. This is a true kingdom ministry! This happened because of the generous kindness of our First Church partners. You know who you are.

- I was able to give a generous tip to a waitress today that needs our prayers. Pray with me for Rhonda today. Thank you for allowing me to be your pastor and for the support you provide for my family that enables me to bless people like Rhonda.

- This Bible School program will impact the community because of the faithful partnership of the generous people in this room. If you are a regular financial partner in this church, thank you. A lot of children are going to find Jesus and be discipled because of your faithfulness. I know that God is going to reward that faithfulness.

QUESTIONS TO PONDER:

1. List your current weekly outline for social media.

2. Social media wise, are you currently everywhere your congregation is?

3. What steps could you take today to be more present with your audience on a daily basis?

4. How could you have incorporated partnership narratives into your last electronic posting?

5. How often do you include financial partnership success stories in your sermons?

6. Has your finance committee identified members of your congregation who could be specifically asked to underwrite a special project?

CHAPTER Nine
ARTICLE - Three Threats

The television, the mailbox, and our beloved computers bring us tragedy on a daily basis. Most everything is a pressing need.

Fighting Compassion Overload

We are in a day where everyone - everywhere is hit with tragic graphics and significant needs. If it is not SPCA's save the dogs and cats, it is Wounded Warrior's save the Vets, or Green Peace's save the ocean. I just found out that mole crickets are on the endangered species list... but obviously not in my yard. Everyone is crying out for money, and we can quickly go to CharityWatch.org and charitynavigator.org and verify the work of our favorite non-profits. Some non-profits spend as much as ninety-seven cents out of every dollar asking for more dollars. These charities are very good at STARPA, and together they can nickel and dime your audience to death.

Encourage people, when they are called by a phone solicitor, to ask what percentage of the donation goes to the charitable organization. They are required to tell you. Often, they will hang up rapidly! In a day where there is contempt for charities, we as ambassadors of good and faithful ministries need to be all the more vocal. We have to lead the charge for good and wise investing among a sketchy brood of people.

"The poor we will always have with us." People deflect giving opportunities with that half-quoted verse every day. Even people who never read the Bible seem to know the first part of that verse. But like most verses, we need to look at the entire context. When Jesus spoke, he quoted from the Duet 15:11 saying, "There will always be poor people in the land. Therefore I command you to be openhanded toward those who are poor and needy." Jesus gave them the full story.

Teach your congregation to fight compassion overload and encourage them to go on local and world mission trips. Demonstrate how to look beyond the televised problem and search for the root cause. Encourage them to fight to keep compassion in their hearts. Teach them to choose a place of purpose where their dollars can make a genuine difference.

In the book *The Whatever Life Hack*, church members are taught to first invest systematically in the local church, then to invest regularly in people around them, and then to find [one] place of significant purpose in the world. They are taught to say "no" to the voices of professional fundraisers on every corner and every television channel.

A wonderfully wise and experienced pastor in South Florida faced the same downturn that every church in the country faced back in 2009. Other churches in his area were laying off staff, and some were close to closing. Arising to the platform and addressing the financial situation (perceived or otherwise) that every member was living through too, he spoke from his faith. "We are not going to live in a defeated mentality in our church. We are going to [out-give] this economic downturn. We are going to add another offering every Sunday and give that offering to missions around the world." It sounded crazy to many, but he had the guts to believe it and live it. While those other churches laid off half of their staff, their church thrived and gave millions of dollars to missions. Stewardship is always a way to fight the good fight of faith. Denying the audience the opportunity to sow and reap (Gal 6:7) is never a Biblical option.

Consumerism

Wikipedia (paraphrased) reminds us that consumerism is a social and economic order and ideology that encourages the acquisition of goods and services in ever-increasing amounts. In the almost complete absence of other sustained macro-political and social narratives —concern about global climate change notwithstanding—the pursuit of the "good life" through practices of what is known as consumerism has become one of the dominant global social forces, cutting across differences of religion, class, gender, ethnicity, and nationality.[39]

"Give me five minutes with a person's checkbook, and I will tell you where their heart is."
- Dr. Billy Graham[40]

We all know the effects of consumerism. We have been serving *Dave Ramsey* and *Crown Financial* material at our churches for years in efforts to deal with the ramifications of our rampant consumerism. How do

[39] https://en.wikipedia.org/wiki/Consumerism
[40] www.brainyquote.com/quotes/billy_graham_385912

we fight it and win? Does our own church staff demonstrate patience in personal buying habits? Do we model conservative spending, or are we known as the people who always have the latest gadget, the newest car, or the most recent iPhone? Sorry if that hit too close to home. When all the dollars are going out the window for disposables, there is little left for the church.

Consumerism is the socially acceptable drug of choice for Christians! Our favorite websites are eBay, Amazon, and Bible Gateway. In that order.

Leaders need to model conservative living. If happiness cannot be achieved outside of the latest gadget, there is little hope for Christianity. Hire people who are modeling the message your marketing.

Political Posturing Problems

Are you teaching your people to make godly decisions and to live biblical ethics in their voting selection? Excellent teaching empowers [the listener] to make the right decisions for themselves.

If we properly teach our congregation right from wrong, and real from forgery, we will not need to micromanage their every political decision. Good teaching brings peace to the teacher. Our own inability to teach well forces us tell our people exactly where to stand on every issue. Welcome to the world of the Cults!

"A leader that does not train his people is just a tour guide." -Larry Osborne[41]

The day in which politics are decided on one or two significant issues is over. As the younger generations grow, you will find that the old significant issues are passing away. Let's illustrate this using abortion as our huge divisive issue. For the record, your authors are very pro-life and raise multi-millions of dollars for pro-life Pregnancy Resource Centers every year.

It used to be that any Christian voted without question for a pro-life candidate. However, one issue voting is not guaranteed anymore. Are God's people not pro-life anymore? For the most part, they [are] still pro-life, but many believe this issue is becoming nothing more than a vote gainer and political money maker. They believe there will be nothing done legislatively about abortion either way, as nothing has been for forty years. They have observed that when the pro-life party has the votes to overturn abortion, they never to take the opportunity until they become outnumbered. Let them become outnumbered, and then they are all screaming about the other side keeping them from doing anything about it. If you tell your congregation to vote for [one party] to see abortion (as our example) overturned, they may silently laugh at your naiveté. They might even begin to question your ability to lead with intelligence.

Unfortunately the [abortion] issue (as our example) has become an integral fundraiser for both

---

[41] https://careynieuwhof.com/episode229/

sides. As long as this fight is creating lots of money for the parties, they will continue to fight for the fight. For the fight, not the solution, is where the consistent money is at.

If we have to tell our people which politicians or policies are good and which are bad, most likely we have not taught them how to think correctly on their own. That is a greater indictment on us as the trained disciple-makers than it is on the panhandling politicians.

Your very conservative, profoundly pro-life authors believe you need to teach your people to separate the truth from the lies themselves, so when you are gone, they will be able to walk in truth and righteousness. Teach your people how to make godly decisions and avoid naming enemy parties (see Exodus 23:13). There are a lot of good people who wear both red or blue, especially on the local level. There are [bad] people on both sides of the political aisle too. Politic preaching will divide your congregation and cost you donations. Politics has always been a pay-to-play game, whether you are in it personally or speaking about it from a high-top coffee table with a brass plaque attached.

"How do you know when a politician is lying? His mouth is open."
-Jay Leno, Comedian[42]

---

[42] https://www.thetimes.co.uk/article/so-how-do-you-know-a-politician-is-lying-when-his-lips-move-2hsnm8z6359

The word politics is derived from two words.
Poly, which means many, and ticks,
which are blood sucking creatures.

Recently a pastor added a to our conversation. He reminded us that the Pharisees linked with the power of the day (Caesar Augustus and King Herod) to retain their own semblance of power and tradition. They ended up being much corrupted in doing so. Their fear of Jesus was in part related to how the Roman power structure might treat their own sect because of His messianic declarations. Ultimately, the answer to national morality is not held in the hands of politicians. Transformation lies not in legislation but the heart. The church is to be the salt and light in a community that delivers a message of transformation. Be careful placing your hand in the hand of any Herod.

Gospel Goes Green

The younger parishioners care deeply about the Earth. They may not buy into global warming, but they have observed climate change. They believe in doing something to improve air quality in our cities. They believe in creating cleaner water for the third world and their own hometown. They are the most earth-friendly demographic history has ever seen since Adam. The post-modern sees Earth as belonging to the Lord, and they desire to protect His property as we would want to protect the church property. Who is more right? Is brick and mortar of more value than rivers and mountains? God spoke on mountains more than He ever spoke in temples. The churches will burn one day too. Do we want to battle the greener mindset? Is that what we were called by God to change, climate voters? *With a world in need of the glorious gospel, shall we fight the tree hugging Toyota Prius drivers first?*

Simply put, the younger audience does not see one political party as a great God-ordained party. They see the abuses of power. Many see Jesus and their faith in a less political light. They look for a Savior who will bring justice for the poor, deliver the captives, care for the widows and orphans (Luke 4:17-19 / Isaiah 42:1). Again, do we want to battle this mindset in our sermon narratives? Is our American version of capitalism what we were called by God to promote? What will be our proof texts or that?

We must decide if we are distributing the faith of our political parties or the faith of our Savior. One will draw the world unto Himself, and the other will use our influence to obtain money and votes. Political posturing will cost you in the offering plate. *There is a price to pay for everything we support.*

QUESTIONS TO PONDER:

1. Do you believe media is creating compassion overload in your audience?
2. How does the lifestyle of your church staff model a conservativeness in your financing?
3. What trust level do you have in those you have mentored for years?
4. Do you teach your congregation what to think, or how to think rightly for themselves?

5. Does it matter whether or not someone believes in climate change?

6. Should the church use LED bulbs to show their energy conservativeness?

7. Should the church promote recycling to reduce garbage in our landfills?

CHAPTER TEN
Article - Earn Your Support

Show me the results! As stewards of resources that God has provided, we are responsible to make sure that we are distributing it properly. To raise money effectively is only half the battle. If we harvest a million dollars in a worthwhile godly way and let it squandered, or wasted it ourselves, we are bad stewards.

"I support a mission in the Dominican Republic that I can go and visit and see their work. I want to know they are accomplishing the work my financial support is providing. To not observe due diligence is to forsake my job as a steward of the resources God has entrusted to me."
- Bob Lash, Automotive Dealer

Imagine for a moment you are the [former] pastor of your church. Knowing what you know about the finances of the church, and how they are stewarded, could you ethically give ten percent of your income to this church based on their inner office stewardship and missional success? If the answer is not an affirmative one, reverse the tables again. You are now back in leadership. Create the church you would support. Remember, you are not only the fundraising leader, you are the one who will be held responsible by God for the way that His money flowed through your authoritative hands. *Do you believe that you will be held accountable by God for your leadership?* I often wonder if the works (good/bad/benign) our churches fund could pass a God audit? *Would our works be accused of the same kind of pork-belly projects that we condemn the political world for having?*

Is the baptismal pool dry rotting? Is the church reaching their neighborhood with the good Gospel? Has everyone in a mile circle around your church had the good news shared with them by a member of the church leadership multiple times? Do the programs offered transform lives, or do they fill spots on the weekly calendar? Is there anything on your website calendar other than Sunday service times? (NOTE: If your online calendar makes your church look boring - get rid of the online calendar. If you don't have anything to list, don't make a list.)

> *"Just because you put the words 'International Ministries' on the side of your doublewide and have an internet video channel, does not mean you have an international ministry. There is a Siamese cat on YouTube that has raised a lot more money for third-world projects than you. Get real."*
> *- Paul Aldrich, Comedian[43]*

Be the pastor you would support. Is your work ethic demonstrative of someone who is driven to make a difference? Have you modeled evangelism to your congregation? Are your associates always there to represent you because you are never available? Do you and your spouse participate in the everyday service

---

[43] www.PaulAldrich.com

ministries of the church even if there is nobody there to observe it? *People are watching.*

Staph or Staff Infection?

Are your staff members known as servants of the people? Do your associate pastors spend every dollar of their budget, even on items not needed, to make sure they don't lose that budget amount next year? *God forbid.* Are your staff members eleven percent givers?

What does your church secretary genuinely think of the staff? We talk to secretarial staff (executive assistants) every day. You can read their negative vocal inflection and their disdain at repeatedly covering for the person they represent.

If you can be trusted with very little, you can also be trusted with much. If you are dishonest with very little, we have reason to question your handling of much. If you have not been trustworthy in handling worldly wealth, can God trust you with true riches? If you have not been trustworthy with someone else's property, should you have property of your own? -Luke 16:10-12 para

But There Is More

Are your leadership eleven percent givers? Are they generous? When was the last time the elders, deacons, and finance committee fasted a full day for the church finances or the congregational finances? *Let's put that one on the calendar for next week.* You might find out who is in it to win it, and who is in it for the ego or control. *When asking these hard questions verbally, always keep your resume ready.*

Bottom line, we are all working for God Himself. God provides for us through the banking portal of the local church checking account, but we will have our life's review one day with God, not the church. May we all be able to stand before Him having done our absolute best for His church, His people, and His world.

QUESTIONS TOP PONDER:

1. Knowing all you know, if you were a member of your congregation, and felt no Biblical mandate to give 10% of your income, would you consider your church a wise investment?

2. Could you, as CEO of your church or organization, stand before God today with a clear conscience that you have protected frivolous spending as an exemplary steward of His funds?

3. Divide your church operating budget by the number of people you have in the seats each week. What is the cost per person to run your operation?

CHAPTER ELEVEN
Connecting For Rapid Results

What good is excellent information if it's just fodder for a rousing game of religious trivial pursuit? We will close with the most straightforward, most attainable, and congealable recap of the articles. Mastering these axioms leaves you fully equipped to generate more significant income for your church and foster greater discipleship of systematic partnership (tithing) in those you lead.

Fear No More

We recognize that we are in the midst of a multi-generational, post-modern theology shift, where everything is legal through grace. Thus the mindset of our culture may consider tithing (legalistic or not) to be optional. We will not shy away from talking about systematic giving. We choose to give our audience the full counsel of God. We will not let the charlatans control the narrative of Biblical giving.

Multi Linguistic Approach

We understand the very word tithing is so Old English that many people can't understand or articulate the meaning. We will find culturally relevant words to disciple people to systematic partnership and shareholding in the work of the local church.

Trustworthy

We recognize our need to create an environment of genuine trust. That will be the foundation upon which our systematic giving can and will be taught. We will be leaders worthy of trust.

Creative Celebration

We will refuse to let the offering times be the most mundane or stagnant part of our service. We will not play instrumental music that only moves the hearts of the elderly. The music we use for these offering times will be the best and most inspirational of the day. We will not be limited to music as the only backdrop for the offering. We will bring multi-media presentations to our offering times. We will make the offering time to be a high note in the service. We will orchestrate the offering to be a celebration as if this were a joyful sacrament because it is.

Positive Prepared Prayer

We will not let the most annoying voices, nor the least prepared voices lead the offertory prayer. We will include in our offering prayers great thanksgiving to God for the faithful partners who cause results to happen and thank God for the opportunity to give. We understand that we are not praying [for] an offering, we are dedicating our gifts to God in thanksgiving. We are thanking God for His promised blessing upon our financial partnership (tithes).

Give Time For Preparation

We will not rush the offering time or hide it in embarrassment. We will give our audience time to seek God and contemplate their giving. We will create thought- provoking times to bless God in celebration of giving. We will not rush from the prayer to plate passing.

Articulate Significance

We will preface each and every corporate giving opportunity by sharing a tangible way a donor's gift made a successful impact the previous week. We will inspire our audience to participate in greatness. We understand people give because they want to be a part of something significant. We will keep successes attached to every offering. We understand that donors want and need to be a hero. We will offer our financial partners a chance to be the hero of the results of their gift. This requires great humility on our part.

If, and even though we are fully electronic in our giving, we will continue to offer times in every service to inspire our members in their electronic giving.

Narrate Concisely

We will create short, well-crafted, five-line passionate narratives declaring [why] funding is needed and [how] their investment will be a solution. We will learn to articulate rapidly so as not to distract the listener in the fog of mundane detail. When dealing with special projects we will share the need and an exact dollar amount needed to eliminate the need.

Tie It Together

We will craft our partnership and hero narratives into all of the messages of the church, including our sermons, newsletters, blogs, and tweets to develop a greater passion for financial stewardship. We will have continuity of message.

Going Viral

We will articulate the effectiveness of our work in every narrative, showing that our church or mission is worthy of being sponsored. From our newsletters and Facebook posts to our Instagram account, we are always carefully creating the right atmosphere for financial partnership inspiration without appearing desperate or greedy. We are not money hungry. We are hungry for teaching the biblical discipline of tithing and financial partnership to every generation. We are hungry to fully fund the great commission and the mission of our church.

We will use our electronic media to speak to our people daily. We will not complain about the limited time with our people, because we have all the time we need with them because we use the media God has given to us. We will use our electronic communications early each week to prep our congregation for great partnership giving.

Multiple Plates

We understand that we are in the electronic culture. We will be prepared to receive offerings and tithes in traditional and contemporary ways. We will not let the ease of electronic giving delete our time to inspire investors.

Voice Thanksgiving

We will find creative ways to repeatedly thank the church partners in sermons, newsletters, personal letters, texts, and telephone calls. Our deacons, elders, and church staff will aid in this individual articulation of honor for the giving partner. We have observed the power of giving thanks to both God and the donor. We realize that we can never thank a donor too many times.

Good Value

We will be worth supporting. We will not abuse a single dollar of God's money. We accept our responsibility to manage God's money and will use our more significant income for a useful purpose. We will know from year to year the per person cost of our ministry.

Special Projects

We will articulate special projects through a STARPA presentation. We will SHOW the need, TELL the exact amount needed, ASK for an immediate gift, RESPOND rapidly with thanksgiving, and PROVIDE proof of project completion. Because of this we will able to ASK again for the next project without hesitation. When sharing special projects, we will always include an exact amount it will take to meet that need. There will be no second round of asking as a result of our miscalculations!

> *You cannot fool God, so don't make a fool of yourself! You will harvest what you plant.*
> *-Galatians 6:7 CEV*

One More Song For You

We are excited about your financial future. You can improve your tithes and offerings. Will it take work? Yes. Anything of value does. These axioms work. We have used them successfully to raise millions and millions of dollars, often in a single weekend. These axioms are not a replacement for prayer and fasting. Neither is prayer and fasting an alternative for preparation.

Use those increased tithes to genuinely impact the world for the kingdom of God. We have put our time—and years of experience in producing this material for you. Use it properly. Stir up the gifts.

CHAPTER TWELVE
Get Brave!

Understanding the mindset and the motivational triggers in a donors mind is only the beginning. By all means, it is not the end all. We have a Biblical mandate to teach tithing and/or intentional investing to the flock. It is Biblical! We must not ever shy away from the Bible.

Is God good? Does He care about our daily lives? What if God required His people to tithe to teach them the amazing results of His Law of Intentional Joyful Investing? What if sowing and reaping was a gift from God to mankind? Can God educate and prove to us His blessings through our faithful partnership with Him? –The Whatever Life Hack (Renovate Publishing).

When we look back to those noted tithing verses in Malachi, it is interesting how the prophet declares people who have strayed from God can return to Him. He declares in the narrative voice of God that they can return and be [restored] through their giving. Was that too much to pull from those verses? At a minimum, the prophet declares that a sign of their backslidden condition is clearly demonstrated in their lack of financial investment in God's house.

I the Lord never change. Because of that you have not been destroyed. Ever since the time of your ancestors you have consistently turned from my decrees. Return to me, and I will return to you.

Return to me in tithes and offerings. You and your whole nation are under a curse because you are thieves. Bring the whole tithe into the storehouse, that there may be food in my house. Test me in this, and see if I will not throw open the floodgates of heaven and pour out so much blessing that there will not be room enough to store it. I will prevent pests from devouring your crops, and the vines in your fields will not drop their fruit before ripe. Then all the nations will call you blessed, for yours will be a delightful land," says the Lord Almighty.
-Malachi 3:6-12 para

There is no shame in teaching tithing, grace giving, or intentional joy-filled investing. Stewardship is foundational to the walk of every God chaser and Christ follower. But knowing what you now know about this culture, the way in which you articulate this teaching is critical. *Be wise... not unemployed!*

If you can't fix stupid, then maybe you shouldn't waste your effort on that demographic.

We choose to teach Biblical stewardship as a [secret] that [wise] people will desire to be a part of. We teach from the perspective of God's pre-ordained blessings that come from giving, rather than his personalized curse that comes from not giving.

"God is not looking toward Earth to find cheapskates to punish. God has instilled laws of planting and harvesting into all of creation at the

time of creation. Like gravity, these joyful investment laws work for Jews or Gentiles, brown or beige, even lost or saved. When we invest joyfully in His place (the church), His people (others in need), and His purposes (mission minded worldview) we receive His return on our investments. And be it known that God pays a really competitive interest rate."
- The Whatever Life Hack (Renovate Publishing)

We choose to teach the [opportunity] for the investor to experience a natural law that God has ordained into creation. This law of planting and harvesting is as real as the Law of Gravity.

...for whatsoever a man plants, that shall he also harvest. - Galatians 6:7b

Paul got into greater detail in 2 Corinthians as he laid out the plan of intentional investing with a joyful heart. Paul declared that our joy-filled investments gained us a return on our investment type here, an increased return on our investment in eternity, the significance that comes from knowing we made a difference, a group of committed prayer partners, and the glorification of God.

Remember this... a farmer who plants only a few seeds will harvest a small crop. But the one who sows generously will receive a bountiful crop. You must each decide in your heart how much to plant. And don't plant reluctantly or in response to pressure. For God loves a person who gives cheerfully. And God will generously respond with all you need. Then you will always have everything you need and plenty left over to share with others. As the Psalmist penned, "They share freely and give generously to the poor. Their good deeds will be remembered forever." For God is the one who provides seed for the farmer who becomes his bread. In the same way, God will provide for you and increase your resources, and produce a great harvest of repeated generosity in you. Yes, you will be enriched in every way so that you can always be generous. And when we take your gifts to those who need them, they will thank God. So two good things will result from this ministry of giving—the needs of the believers will be met, and they will joyfully express their thanks to God. As a result of your sharing, they will give glory to God for your generosity to them. This will prove that you are obedient to the Good News of Christ. And they will pray for you with deep affection because of the overflowing grace God has given to you. Thank God for this investment gift! -2 Corinthians 9:6-15 para

The book *The Whatever Life Hack* outlines this material in enormous detail from a conservative viewpoint. This is not a name it - claim it self-ology. There is a massive amount of scripture regarding our joyful intentional planting, God's watering, and the well blessed harvest. Jesus was not afraid to talk about money and possessions. Paul was not afraid to declare that God had established laws of planting and harvest.

The Old Testament prophets didn't retreat the subject! We must not be fearful either.

> *The Bible speaks very plainly about money because our hearts and our wallets are tightly bound up together, and God is after our hearts. Jesus used money and possessions as an illustration in 16 of His 38 parables. Matthew, Mark, Luke, and John, contain 288 verses... one out of ten verses deal directly with money. The Bible offers 500 verses on prayer, 500 verses on faith, but more than 2,000 verses on money and possessions.*
> *-Howard Dayton, Crown Financial Ministries*[44]

Intelligently and culturally teach intentional Biblical investing to your people and watch the law of God come into effect on their life, and thus on your church. The rising tide raises every ship in the harbor. Rising stewardship raises the blessings of everyone close to it. Thanks be unto God for his beautiful plan for our lives. This generation is looking for life hacks. Give them the life hack of Biblical stewardship. Give them the life hack of sewing and reaping.

> *Thank God for this investment gift!*
> *-2 Corinthians 9:15 para*

---

[44] www.Crown.org

CHAPTER THIRTEEN
Critical Resources

Small Group Giving Study

The Whatever Life Hack (Renovate Publishing) book is ready to teach your congregation the joys of systematic giving from a very Biblical and culturally relevant approach. *This book is scripture after scripture.* You can Biblically inspire your small group to be systematic givers. Each chapter contains easy to understand group led questions. This book will also serve as an inspiring outline for any sermon series on tithing and biblical investing. Order today at www.amazon.com.

Large Group Generosity Catalyst Events

In addition to their fundraising event schedule, Mike G. Williams and Jack Eason speak at local churches to proclaim the joys and blessings of systematic church shareholding partnerships (tithing). If you would like help in teaching systematic partnership to your congregation, let either of your authors present the *Three Secret Biblical Investments* at your church?[45]

---

[45] See More about Mike G. Williams at MikeWilliams.TV
See more about Jack Eason at www.TheHeartShareGroup.com

Free Illustrations For You

If you are looking for tithing/partnership story narratives and clean humor for your newsletters and social media posts, please request the quarterly Pastor's Humor & Illustration newsletter. Send your newsletter request to mike@CupsMission.com.

A Successful Mission Partnership

Your purchase of this book is a great blessing on a larger scale. The author profits from this book impacts the life of children. A small town in the Dominican Republic is plagued tonight by American males who are there to rob very young girls of their innocence. Changing the world is simple. Together we can fight human trafficking successfully. Come and spend a week and be part of the transformation. Join a successful mission team at www.CupsMission.com.

Organizational Assistance

The HeartShare Group offers on-site donor development strategy for churches and para-church organizations wishing to optimize their income potential. See www.TheHeartShareGroup.com.

Small Group Tithing Video

Rich Praytor Productions has brought to our table a wonderful movie that catalogs a young single mother who decides to take her Pastor's challenge to tithe for 90 days. This is a documentary worth distributing to everyone in your congregation. This is a very culturally relevant production. See www.titheprojectmovie.com.

Historic Tithing Video

Dynamic Kernels Tithing Experiment is a historically interesting video documentary cataloging the tithing experiment of Perry Hayden and Henry Ford. Though these videos are very dated and culturally disconnected, their retro look may be quite appealing and inspirational.
See Dynamic Kernels Tithing Experiment at https://youtu.be/-EP2qrQf5p0.

Larger Offering Plates

Maybe it is time you ordered some larger offering plates. https://www.christianbook.com/large-offering-pot

Maybe it is time you ordered some electronic giving portals. We will let you find these on your own.